***Creative
Loneliness***

William E. Hulme

36

Creative Loneliness

A Christian Counselor
Helps You Live
with Yourself and Others

AUGSBURG PUBLISHING HOUSE
Minneapolis, Minnesota

Contents

Preface

I began gathering ideas for this venture four years ago when I was asked to write a book about loneliness. I then viewed loneliness as an internal problem of identity and placed little emphasis on relationships with other people.

Before I began to write, my family and I experienced the sudden death of my oldest daughter. The editor offered to release me from my writing obligations, and, preoccupied with my bereavement, I accepted. In my cosmic loneliness, I had neither the energy nor the interest to pursue the project.

My views on loneliness changed during this period. I came to regard my previous position as too self-sufficient. In my grief I deeply needed people, and I sought more intimate involvement with others.

As the months have become years I have moved again —this time to a mediating position. I again believe that loneliness is a problem of personal identity, but I also believe that intimacy with others is part of this identity. When I was invited again to write on the subject of loneliness, I was ready. This time I was not simply responding to a request; I sincerely desired to write this book. I do not know how much different it is from the book I would have written four years ago, but I am sure it reflects the influence of the intervening years.

CHAPTER 1

We Are All Lonely

Sarah asked for an appointment because, in her own words, she was "going to pieces." As she expressed her feelings, I saw a frightened, depressed, confused young woman. "I wonder, really, if I can go on," she said. "And that's scary!"

Sarah was alone in the city. Like many others her age, she had come to the big city from a small town to get a job. But she was not ready. She was working in a large office where the impersonal atmosphere diminished her confidence. To her disappointment, she found little opportunity to develop work friendships that would extend beyond the office. After work there was only the loneliness of her very small apartment. Loneliness brought her to her present turmoil.

At an office party, Sarah met a young man who offered to take her home. This was followed by a date, after which they snacked at her apartment. When the time came for him to leave, Sarah saw the spectre of an empty apartment with its closing-in walls. Impulsively, she asked him to stay. He moved in with her, and for a while her pains of loneliness were eased. But he was unstable, and stress mounted between them.

Sarah came from a Christian home. She began to feel guilty about living with the young man. Following a quarrel, she shared her misgivings and asked him to leave. He left, stating that he would not be back. His angry taunt stayed with her: "If you really feel guilty, why did you ask me to move in in the first place!"

"Do you want him to return?" I asked.

"In my saner moments," she said, "I'm actually relieved it's over. But I'm alone again, and the weekend is coming up. Weekends are the worst—especially the nights. I can hardly bear to think of more lonely weekend nights. I know now why I invited him to stay. If he asks to come back, I know what I *should* say—but *will* I?"

Unlike Sarah, Bill stayed in the small town in which he was reared. He worked as a laborer in the small factory on the edge of town. Bill talked a lot, but people didn't pay much attention. In fact, he thought at times they were avoiding him. Bill was hypersensitive to slights and especially to criticism, which he received at times from his boss. Turned inward by keen awareness of his own hurts, Bill was strangely unaware of why he was turning others off.

"I'm lonely," he said to his pastor. "I would like to get married. But girls don't seem to want me—or at least not the ones I want." The pastor observed how even people in the congregation listened with strained politeness to Bill as he talked—often incessantly—while they looked about as though searching for an escape. His forceful approach, though meant to be friendly, was an obstacle to meeting his own needs. Obviously Bill could not be accused of not trying; he was trying too hard. Consequently he was insensitive to the needs and desires of others.

Young, single people are not the only ones who suffer from loneliness. Tom was married, middle-aged, and a very successful corporation executive. He was "in control" of his feelings and "in charge" at his job. He and his wife had gone their own ways, he finding meaning in work and she in community responsibilities. Because they were well-to-do, cultured, and extremely competent, they commanded prestige in their respective settings.

If Tom had any fears, doubts, or weaknesses, he kept them well hidden behind his tough, pragmatic exterior. But then he became ill—terminally ill. His wife asked that he not be told, fearing his response to something he could not handle, combat, or conquer. But Tom suspected the truth. One morning a nurse discovered him in tears. "Am I going to die?" he asked. He was facing the most lonely of experiences and his past ways of coping were of no help. He was frightened, and like a frightened child, he felt all alone.

Tom had been lonely before, but he so thoroughly repressed his feelings that his loneliness was not discernible even to himself. It broke out once, though, through a vulnerable spot in his armor. He became attracted to a woman business associate. With the help of some wine at a late evening business engagement, he began to share with her his need for someone he could talk with and be close to. Tom wanted to continue the relationship as an affair, but she refused. A woman of conviction, she believed the relationship should go no further. So Tom retreated behind his tough exterior, defending his wounded pride by again denying his unsatisfied need. He threw himself even more passionately into his work.

Many feel lonely when a significant relationship ends. Widows, widowers, and divorced persons are chief among these; people who lose a parent or a good friend are also included. The needs of such persons are a prime object of Christian concern. As James states in his letter, "Religion that is pure and undefiled before God and the Father is this: to visit orphans and widows in their affliction" (1:27).

Marie expressed dismay with her widowed mother. "Dad's been gone 10 years now," she said, "and yet Mother is always nattering about how lonely she is. She has her health, she drives her own car, she's active at church. Why does she complain so much about being lonely?"

Marie does not realize that none of her mother's advantages replaces a soul mate. At night her mother is alone —all alone. Memories return of the time she was not alone and she grieves for lost intimacy.

I recall after my father became widowed, when he talked on the phone or wrote a letter, he would always volunteer, "I'm all by myself now—I'm so lonesome."

Loss of a mate through divorce is complicated by mixed feelings. Yet the divorced person experiences the same predicament as the widowed: former friends no longer know how to "fit them in." As one such person put it, "Old couple friends don't know what to do with me, it seems. I don't fit in with their groups now that I'm single, unless they can think of some other single person to couple me with. And that can be most awkward. We newly singled persons seem destined slowly but surely to be dropped from their social calendars. We no longer belong."

As age adds its increased limitations and confinements, the loneliness and isolation can become even worse. An older person may be confined largely to the "company" of television characters. Not only is it difficult for the elderly to get out of their houses or apartments because of reduced mobility and transportation; it may not even be safe if the neighborhood has grown old with them. One such oldster was desperate enough in her loneliness to place an ad in the personal column of her newspaper. "My phone has not rung in two weeks. Is anybody still out there? If so please call me—for I'm so very lonely. I need to talk with *somebody*." She received many calls as a result, but how many thousands like her do not have the temerity to take such initiative?

All of us, from youth to the aged, can understand one another in our loneliness. Even children know the pain. In fact, loneliness may have its roots in childhood. Children who are teased and tormented by siblings or peers feel attacked and may withdraw. Children whose parents are preoccupied with their own problems and troubles can feel shut out and alone. When parents quarrel, children's anxiety is intensified because they fear the parents may hurt each other or even abandon each other— and the children.

Ironically, all indications are that loneliness is increasing right along with the population explosion. Certainly loneliness is not caused by lack of people. Increased numbers of people seem to intensify loneliness. In apartment complexes and high rise buildings, people are stacked together so closely that they hear others quarreling in the adjoining apartment and making love in the apartment above, yet they may not be "neighbors" to anyone.

The Need for Intimacy

Because of our human nature, we all need intimate relationships. We live together in families, tribes, and communities not only because we need each other, but also because we enjoy each other's company.

When our need for intimacy is not met, we tend to become depressed, though we may not realize the connection. In our deprivation we feel rejected, walled in by our lonely rooms. We know the pain of loneliness—the ache in the pit of the stomach that zaps morale and depletes energy.

Many seek to ease this pain by compensating with activities. One of the most common diversions is work. Our culture is production-oriented rather than relationship-oriented, so work is a natural substitute for intimate relationships, particularly for people whose work is sufficiently creative to permit an unlimited investment of time and energy.

A physician describing psychosomatic ills told how he resolved his own psychosomatic pains. During Sundays spent with his family, he developed recurring headaches which he concluded were psychosomatic. When he went to his office Sunday afternoons, the headaches ceased. By such adjustments to our needs, he said, we can overcome our psychosomatic ills.

Like many others in our society, the physician used

work to meet most of his needs—particularly his need for closeness with others. He adjusted to deprivations of closeness by compensations he derived from his job. He had become addicted to work and his headaches were withdrawal symptoms. He felt tense when confronted with family intimacy. Even as sunlight may hurt the eyes of those accustomed to darkness and abundant food may make ill a person accustomed to scanty rations, so opportunity for intimacy may create unanticipated anxiety among those unaccustomed to closeness with others. By uncritically pursuing his medical goal of eliminating pain, the physician missed the opportunity to endure such pain until he became at ease with intimacy.

Work is often referred to as good therapy, and it is. It is also a good hiding place. In our competitive culture, work supplies opportunities for ego-building. We can establish a sense of value and importance by achievements at work. But the addict routes into work the energies normally devoted to intimacy and caring. Work then becomes a substitute satisfaction for our need for closeness and love.

Work, of course, is not the only compensation for lack of intimacy. The most common addiction, alcoholism, is also related to loneliness. Alcohol produces within us sensations we would experience through intimacy with other people. The addict feels "high" or "good" or "relaxed." People in bars often appear to be very sociable, yet an acquaintance of mine who frequents bars describes them as "dens of loneliness." The need for chemical stimulation to facilitate sociability indicates that at least some of this sociability is superficial.

This is particularly true when the effects of alcohol become obvious. A person feeling high believes he or she is "freed up" to communicate. But a recent study has corrobated the common observance that persons whose tongues are loosened by alcohol not only talk more freely but also listen very poorly. They interrupt those with whom they are speaking, tend to be disorganized and repetitive in their speech, and are generally boring if not boorish. Such socializing is a palliative for the pains of loneliness, but scarcely a cure.

Some lonely people resort to promiscuity because sex provides a semblance of intimacy. Yet promiscuous sex, instead of mediating intimacy, caring, and loving, is a superficial substitute. While sex between caring people communicates great intimacy, sex between strangers accentuates isolation. As with alcohol and other drugs, when the stimulation subsides, little remains to obscure loneliness.

Lonely people are vulnerable to addiction, whether to work, alcohol, drugs, or promiscuous sex. The addiction temporarily alleviates pain. Frustrations over loneliness are blocked out by compensatory satisfactions. Addicts prefer fleeting gratification to facing up to the imbalance in their lives, even as elderly persons with no meaningful role in society may prefer the illusions of senility to an empty existence. Such people may not consciously miss the comfort and ecstasy of intimate relationships. But the compensation of addiction comes at high cost.

It would seem to be a law of nature that when something is lacking, imbalance necessitates a corresponding compensation. We human beings, however, differ from the rest of nature by our potential for making decisions. Instead of instinctively compensating for our deprivations to rectify the imbalance, we can deal with them directly. If you are lonely, you can do something other than compensate—you can confront your loneliness directly. Like the elderly woman who put an ad in the newspaper, you can take steps to alleviate loneliness. The purpose of this book is to assist you.

Loneliness is widespread, but is it a normal human condition? Is it a symptom of more basic problems? Is it related to other needs? We must explore these and other questions to cope intelligently with this problem. Hopefully if we raise the right questions, we can come up with workable answers.

CHAPTER 2

To Be Human Is to Be Lonely

Human beings, it is assumed, are differentiated from other forms of life by self-consciousness. Besides being aware of bodily sensations and what is going on in our environment, we are also aware of ourselves as beings distinct and separate from others. I can refer to myself as *I* or *me* depending on whether I am the subject or observer of my actions. Self-consciousness makes us acutely aware not only of our uniqueness, but also of our aloneness. Loneliness begins with the dawn of self-consciousness.

The uniqueness of each human being is an observable, scientific fact. Identification by fingerprinting symbolizes this uniqueness. Awareness of our own uniqueness, however, is highly subjective. Our often painful perception of our borders, of our difference from others, is the natural basis for loneliness.

This individuality we each experience creates tension

within community living. Tribal existence minimized this conflict by submerging individuality to group identification. Ancient peoples, however, still produced individuals. One of the most painful descriptions of separated existence is that of Job in the Old Testament. Modern living obviously has accentuated this sense of separateness. The loss of community is a by-product of urbanization. Modern individuals feel lost in the mass. They experience their uniqueness mostly through loneliness.

Our physical borders also express our uniqueness. No two people, not even identical twins, look exactly alike. Our bodies also define our boundaries; they confine and protect our individuality. We are limited to a particular space and time.

Yet we are not confined to our bodies. When my children were small I often engaged them in a ritual game of identification. "Who are you?" I would ask. "I'm me," the child would respond. "Who's me?" I asked. The child would point to some part of his body and say, "This is me." "No," I would say, "that's your arm." The child would try again. "This is me!" "No, that's not you, that's your chest. Where are *you?*" In frustration the child would say, "I don't know."

If the ritual had any point, it was to impress on the child the complexity of his own existence: he was more than his tangible body; he was also spirit or consciousness. However, when the child tried to identify his spirit apart from his body, he was stumped. So am I! So, I imagine, are you! We know we are identified with our bodies: they give us pain and pleasure. When I cut my finger my whole being experiences the pain; when I enjoy sex my whole being experiences the pleasure. Yet I can also leave my body. With my imagination I can travel in space and time, while my body remains stationary.

I can also use my body to hide my spirit. I can pretend I am asleep when I am awake. I can smile when I am hostile. I can look calm when I am scared. The profession of acting is devoted to such body manipulation. Some animals also have this faculty. The oppossum feigns death to discourage its would-be molesters. But the oppossum acts instinctively for survival, while human beings are aware of playacting. They can reflect on it—even feel guilty about it. When we use our bodies to hide our identity, we show how little our bodies really confine us. Rather than liberating our spirits, however, transcendence may only increase our sense of isolation and loneliness.

Our ability to transcend our bodies has its limitations. Bodies are subject to injury, illness, and degeneration. Ultimately they bring us to the loneliest of all experiences —death. Though all of us die, each dies alone. Animals also die, but unlike animals we are *aware* we will die. Consequently we fear death, protest it. Fear of death adds to our loneliness. Yet our bodies' confinement of our individuality is not absolute even in death. Human beings have hoped to survive death as long as we have recorded history. Religious rituals and revelations have supported this hope. Despite these supports, the hope for life after death remains just that—a hope. Scientific evidence is lacking. Human beings have good reason to be lonely.

Loneliness as Pain

Loneliness is a psychic pain—a dread in the depths of one's being. Its origin is in the separateness of our uniqueness and the alienation that may ensue. Perhaps at times you have felt so different from others that you experienced virtually no contact with them. Henry David Thoreau knew this sense of differentness. He defended it by saying, "If a man does not keep pace with his companions, perhaps it is because he hears a different drummer."

We may be most conscious of the pain of separateness at night. Darkness seems to symbolize the dread we feel. Nights when one has difficulty sleeping are probably worst of all. The biggest problem with insomnia is the anguish it produces. A father recently bereaved by the sudden death of his son put it this way: "I usually go to sleep when I retire. I guess I'm just exhausted. But I wake up in about three or four hours and that's it. I can't get back to sleep, and those long night hours are pure agony. By the time morning finally comes, I've had it!"

A person who wakes in the quiet of the night is most vulnerable to the influence of the subconscious mind. Disturbing dream symbols leave their emotional imprint. The defenses intact during the day are lowered. Even when we are not experiencing stress so obvious as that of the bereaved father, traumas buried in our subconscious make us vulnerable to anxiety.

We experienced separation as infants, long before events were recorded in our memories. Early traumas left their imprint and they affect us as adults. This is especially disturbing because we have no explanatory memories.

Separation Built into Life Cycle

The experience of separation begins at birth. An infant leaves the warmth and quiet of its mother's womb and enters the world as a separate being—a shock, perhaps a severe trauma. The influence of this experience on the infant's development is difficult to assess. Psychoanalyst Otto Rank believed the birth trauma to be the crucial experience for all of life. He weakened his case by tracing all of our ills to this source. In recent times Dr. Frederick Leboyer, a French obstetrician, has pioneered minimizing the shock of birth. "The newborn is a sensitive feeling human being," he states, "and in the first few moments after birth, he should be treated that way. We must introduce the baby into the world gradually." [1] His methods purportedly bring babies into the world smiling rather than crying. While it is too soon to be sure, indications are that these children may be emotionally more positive than their crying-baby counterparts.

After the birth separation, many children enter a family including other children who threaten to separate the newcomer even more from his or her parents. In adolescence the child experiences a heightened sense of individuality, with painfully self-conscious moments of embarrassment. During puberty, physical development creates a drive toward intimacy which is at odds with the young person's acute sense of separation. Marriage may intensify this tension. While we are drawn to marriage to satisfy our need for intimacy, we may also be frightened by the threatened curb of our uniqueness, wondering whether our individuality will be smothered. This familiar double mind is the basis for much of the marital disruption prevalent in our day.

During mid-life the end of life comes ominously into view, and the conflicts of adolescence are resurrected. Previous goals and supports are discarded, bringing a heightened sense of uniqueness and separateness. Old age is a time of increasing losses—of health, position, sensory perceptions, mobility, and loved ones. Older people often feel set apart, outside the mainstream of life, and the loneliness created by such losses can be most painful.

The Loneliness of Traumas

While potential for loneliness is built into the successive stages of our development, we experience loneliness most acutely in times of deep sorrow and trouble. Grieving over the loss of loved ones, for example, brings a very lonely anguish. When our oldest daughter was taken from us in sudden death, friends reached out to us. They wanted to share our grief. "I can't take the pain away," said one of them, "but I can walk with you in it." But he and we knew that he could only go so far—and then we had to go on alone. Differences may exist even in the manner of grieving. Obviously in the death of a child, father and mother share the same grief. Yet they may feel very separated from each other in the *way* they grieve. "My husband won't talk about it with me," one mother lamented. "I know he's hurt deeply, but he is not one to show his feelings. What separates us even more is that he doesn't want me to talk about it either; he says it doesn't do any good. I feel so alone in my sorrow."

Jesus experienced this loneliness as sorrow in the Garden of Gethsemane. Knowing he faced death the following day, he took his disciples with him to the garden to prepare himself for the ordeal. He chose three of them with whom he shared his deep sorrow. He asked them to remain awake while he prayed. It was *his* trauma—*his* imminent death. Yet he needed his friends to be with him. But they went to sleep instead. When he awakened them, he asked, "Could you not watch with me one hour?"

(Matt. 26:40). But they went to sleep again, and he was left alone.

Yet he was not alone. He was praying. He was in contact with God. When the fearful event arrived, however, even this contact was threatened. "My God, my God," he cried out, "why hast thou forsaken me?" (Mark 15:34). He was experiencing the silence of God. Many years before, another sufferer experienced the same silence. "Oh, that I had one to hear me!" he cried (Job 31:35). Job suffered many ills, but the one which he anguished over most was the hiddenness of God.

In *Turn Over Any Stone* Edna Hong has put this ancient protest of the sufferer into personal expression in a fierce free verse:

> What are you—Creator or Father?
> If Creator,
> are *they* your image?
> Do *you,* then, have a monster head?
> Are *you* hunchbacked, clubfooted?
> Do we worship a Divine Freak?
> Do we pray to a Divine Absurdity,
> a Supernatural Monster?
>
> If Father,
> then what happened to all the fatherly
> virtues: tenderness, protectiveness,
> affection, solicitude?
>
> Answer me, you who claim to be
> both Creator and Father.
> Answer!

But all I got was silence.
I scolded him like a shrew.
I displayed the temper of a female fiend.
I insulted him.
I poured out obscenities
I did not know I had within me.

But he was silent,
and I remembered a verse in a psalm and found it:

"Is he deaf, the God who planted the ear?" [2]

The Swedish motion picture producer Ingmar Bergman has made several films on the theme of the silence, the hiddenness, of God, two examples of which are *The Silence* and *Winter Light.* The depression portrayed in these films spills over into the audience. Obviously Bergman too has experienced this silence and agonized over it, for his films portray brilliantly the loneliness of this frustrating quest. And there they end! Jesus' agony on the cross ended differently. In the midst of the silence, he could still trust: "Father, into thy hands I commit my spirit!" (Luke 23:46). This trust in the midst of silence Bergman seems not to know and therefore cannot portray.

Yet trusting God is as authentic in human experience as sensing his hiddenness. This trust speaks directly to human loneliness. In fact, it bridges it. One can trust because, in spite of the present silence, at some time God has spoken. Although he is hidden, he is also revealed.

We will explore further this breach in human loneliness in a later chapter. Our concern now is to look further into the nature of human loneliness and the distortions in living which complicate it.

CHAPTER **3**

When Loneliness
Gets Out of Hand

Loneliness is more than a normal accompaniment to the events and stages of human life. It is also a consequence of what is wrong about human beings. Many have attempted to describe this wrongness, since it is so plentifully in evidence and it affects us all. We are described as "off-centered" by some, "egocentric" by others. Obviously we have gotten off the track. The biblical word for our state is "fallen," referring to the story in the Book of Genesis about the fall into sin. People are seldom described as sinners any more, except in ancient church rituals. Sin is an "antique" among words, and future dictionaries may list it as archaic.

Resurrecting an Old Word

The demise of the word *sin* has not gone unnoticed. Recently psychiatrist Karl Menninger wrote a book titled

Whatever Became of Sin? The response in sales has been phenomenal. Obviously there is still an interest in the subject, and the fact that a psychiatrist rather than a clergyman resurrected the word is probably an important part of the interest.

We—myself included—have been hesitant to use the word *sin* because of the abuse associated with it. The label *sinner* has proved to be the harshest of judgments, evoking cruel and sadistic punishments. When I imagine a person speaking the word *sin,* he has a grim face and perhaps even clenched teeth. This response to the word has surely jeopardized its use.

Alcoholism, for example, is now described as a disease. Although some theories outline a possible physiological base to alcoholism, the purpose of describing alcoholism as a disease is to change society's attitude toward the alcoholic. If drunkenness, as it was previously called, is regarded as sin, as it was in the past, the drunk merits judgment, not treatment. A sick person is not considered responsible for his condition; he obviously needs treatment. The other side of the coin, however, is that this treatment for the alcoholic stresses his responsibility. He is discouraged from thinking of himself as a victim, even of circumstances, and instead is confronted repeatedly in group therapy with his irresponsible choices which contributed to his predicament.

The Defenses of Egocentricity

According to Christian tradition, sin is defined as self-curved-in-on-itself. We cut ourselves off from others, denying the basic human impulse to reach outward—to God and to others. The closest synonym for sin is egocentricity. The word *ego* is simply the Latin word for *I*. When the self (the I, the ego) curves in on itself, it becomes distorted. This distortion has created a second definition for *ego,* namely, *distorted I.* The words *egotist, eogism,* and *egocentric* are based on this second definition.

What is distorted about the distorted I? In our egocentricity we are suspicious of others. Our capacity to trust has been undermined by what cultural analyst Karen Horney calls *basic anxiety.* We feel alone and vulnerable in a hostile universe. Our defenses are up: we even speak of ourselves as "guarded." We are wary lest others take advantage of us. People seem potential adversaries rather than friends, quick to pounce if they catch a glimpse of our vulnerability. If we reveal who we are, some people would laugh at us. Therefore we presume all people would laugh. The presumption that we are surrounded by potential attackers leads to extremes of loneliness.

If you are like most of us, you fear this kind of humiliation. If you should fall on the ice or trip on a rug, what is your first thought as you lose your balance? I imagine it is, "Is anybody looking?" Even if we're hurt, most of us will bounce back up. Why do we want to give others the impression that we are not hurt? Evidently we fear they'll reject our hurt. It is bad enough to be clumsy and trip or slip, but to get hurt in addition is much harder on our ego. So we bounce up, despite our pain, and try not to limp so those who witness will not say, "Aha!"

Obviously we do not feel we are surrounded by people whom we can trust with our vulnerability. We fear being made to feel like fools. "Ah yes," you may say, "but there are people who *would* laugh!" Right! Because we fear *them* we take no chances with anybody. The flow of our love energy is blocked by this fear and converted instead into the service of our ego. We use our energies in a distorted way to defend ourselves against humiliation. But as any coach knows, the best defense is a good offense. So these energies can be directed toward manipulating, using, and otherwise "conning" others. Our relationships are characterized by power struggles in which each seeks to exercise control—to win—over the other.

This defensive-offensive pose that marks our fallenness is the opposite of sharing, of "opening our hearts." Rather than building bridges to unite us with others, we build walls that separate. Our relationships tend to be superficial, with a great deal of camouflage. Like Adam and Eve, through whom the fall is dramatized, we cannot tolerate being "naked." We need a "covering." The fig leaves they used to cover their nakedness symbolize our attempts to conceal our true selves. The result—intense loneliness!

Guilt and Alienation

A fall does not occur without a reaction. The reaction is guilt. We feel guilty—that is, we are unhappy with ourselves. We sense we are out of line, out of tune, out of harmony. And there is good reason for this discomfort, because we're out of line with our own nature. Yet guilt does not help us get in line—it only makes us suffer for being out of line.

Guilt does more than make us suffer. It makes us disrespect ourselves. In contemporary terms this self-*dis*respect is referred to as a low self-image. We find it difficult to live with the person we are, since we picture

ourselves in an uncomplimentary style. Then guilt
us down into isolation, since it makes us feel uncom.
able in the company of others. Guilt also makes us u
comfortable in our own company, which it is harder to
avoid, though we sometimes make the attempt.

In his New Testament letter, St. James describes how
we are prone to look in a mirror and then forget what
we see. We surround ourselves with distractions, hoping
the memory of the mirror image will go away. These
"forgotten" pictures slip into our subconscious, where
they continue to exert their negative influence. The problem with such "forgetting" is that we are alienated not
only from others, but now also from part of our selves.
Our self-image becomes distorted.

Breakdown of Family Ties

If we human beings are distorted, the social atmosphere
in which we function will also be distorted. The principal
focus of this social distortion is the family. It is bad
enough for an infant to have to leave the dark and quiet
of the womb for separate life in the bright, noisy world,
and even to have to share with siblings what ties remain to
his parents. But if this infant is also deprived of love and
affection because his parents and siblings are egocentric,
his sense of separation is intensified. Small wonder then
that in the course of his existence loneliness can get out
of hand. Sin diminishes the security of family ties because
the more one curves in on oneself, the less one can reach
out in love to others. This "fallen" condition affects all
families and all other human institutions—schools, gov-
ernments, and even churches.

People in nonindustrialized cultures find protection

against basic anxiety by identification with their tribe. The tribe has its enemies, but at least the people are surrounded by nonenemies in the community. In industrialized nations, people lose this tribal identity and become isolated individuals with no supporting groups.

Egocentric people construct a society that fosters alienation and suspicion. In *The Pursuit of Loneliness,* Philip Slater describes how our tendency to engage in power struggles rather than sharing experiences with our neighbors has led us as a society to espouse competition over cooperation, leading to greater loneliness. Good competitors opt for secrecy over openness. They prefer social formalities to authentic expression. How can we live in such competitive isolation without envy, jealousy, and strife—which in turn further insulate us into lonely systems of defense?

A man we'll call Ron was frustrated in both his marriage and his extramarital affair. He found compensating satisfaction in devoting all his energies to work. He was too competitive with men to risk sharing himself with his male colleagues. His work addiction paid off in the ego satisfactions of power and prestige. As a successful competitor, he is in a position *over* others, well fortified against attacks of potential enemies.

But for how long? Not only may another competitor rise to ease him from his safe position, but he himself may some day realize that his addiction is no longer satisfying. Mid-life crises and breakdowns are often brought about by protests from the self hidden behind the fortress. One is faced with the inevitable limits and losses of the aging process. Compulsory retirement looms up forebodingly, and behind it the spectre of increased aging, ill health, loss of abilities and power, and finally death. Then work may cease to be a sufficient outlet for one's energies. The results are anxiety and tension—the usual accompaniments to loneliness gotten out of hand.

Loneliness in Crowds

Ironically, loneliness is characteristic of our huge population centers. We may be packed like proverbial sardines into town houses, condominiums, apartment complexes, and high rises, but the intensity of contact serves only to isolate us. We draw tighter into our shells. Our bodies function as fortresses to conceal and protect the self within. It is no wonder that the bioenergetic school of psychotherapy refers to our "body armor" and concentrates on muscle relaxation for tension release.

As I write this I am living with my family in a second-floor apartment of a 95-unit complex with a population of 350 people. On our side of the street, three larger complexes also stand on our block, for a total population of approximately 2400 people. Perhaps anonymity seems necessary in such high density. Although we have lived here several months, I know few of my neighbors by sight and none by name. People come and go. In the span of two months the neighbors below us and on either side moved. We knew only because of the moving vans and cleanup crews. We hear the people below us and beside us, but we would have difficulty recognizing them by sight. They are like an extended family by sound.

Recently I visited a slum in Tijuana, Mexico, where 7000 squatters live on a small tract of government-owned bottom land. They are crammed together eight people to a shack, yet here I perceive no retreat to anonymity or concern about private space. Perhaps the anonymity is more a phenomenon of apartment living than high density living as such. There is no transciency with these people —they are in the slum to stay. Nor do they have many relationships beyond their living quarters, as do most apartment dwellers. The person who lacks these other relationships will be very lonely in most of our apartment complexes.

We retain our identity in the midst of people by not getting involved with them. The television series "Candid Camera" exploits this noninvolvement for our entertainment. How do people react when confronted by the unexpected? They pretend not to notice or feign noninterest. Why? They are afraid. Once they react honestly they are involved, they are committed, they are vulnerable. Others then can take advantage of them, laugh at them, hurt them.

"Candid Camera" is staged and therefore we can laugh at others and their fear of involvement. But in real life noninvolvement is no laughing matter. We hear all too often of the tragic consequences of this system of defense. Individuals are left to suffer and die while people who could help pretend not to notice. They are so afraid of being hurt themselves that they cannot risk helping others. They hide behind impassive facades. As long as we hide our recognition of what is going on, nothing can be asked of us; we are safe within our fortress.

Though we are more aware of defensive noninvolvement in large cities, loneliness also pervades smaller communities and farmlands. Here also we find people hiding, though their style is different. People in small towns and rural areas interact, but often in guarded, indirect, and superficial ways.

CHAPTER 4

Fear of Intimacy

Many of us are of a double mind about being close to people. On the one hand we long for closeness to ease the misery of loneliness; on the other hand we are afraid of it. In fact, loneliness has been described as fear of love.

Why do we fear love? We are so self-centered that we surround ourselves with defenses, and we are afraid of anything that can penetrate our barricades. Closeness with others threatens to expose our hidden self. Behind our fortress, we are under the illusion that if we become intimately involved we may not be able to extricate ourselves. Actually we fear such closeness will destroy us. The person we permit to enter our fortress could turn out to be a Trojan horse. Once we let him in, it may be too late to protect ourselves from whatever dangers he brings.

In our fortresses we are under the illusion that because we are hidden we are also autonomous. Other people threaten this autonomy. Although we like the *idea* of intimacy and may even become sentimental over it, we may stiffen at its touch, even literally. Have you noticed how quickly some people remove their foot or hand if they accidentally touch your body? They may even apologize for the encounter. Perhaps you yourself have instinctively stiffened or drawn back when somebody—even a friend—touches you, as though the touch violated your privacy. Our tangible bodies symbolize the boundaries of our fortress; even an accidental touch may be taken as a threat of invasion. No wonder an apology seems in order.

The Danish philosopher Soren Kierkegaard saw a connection between resisting intimacy with others and resisting intimacy with God. In *Sickness unto Death,* he illustrated his point with this story: A mighty emperor took a notion to send for a poor day laborer in his realm. The laborer considered himself extremely favored to be privileged just to see the emperor. But it turned out the emperor had much more in mind—he wished to have the laborer for his son-in-law! The laborer understood a small expression of interest, but to marry the emperor's daughter was too much! He lacked the courage to believe the offer. "Such a thing is too high for me, I cannot get it into my head."

Kierkegaard's point is that God makes us a similar offer and we find ourselves in the same consternation. The good news is that he invites us to live on the most intimate terms with him. Yet is this really good news to us? Or do we find ourselves disturbed by it as the day laborer was with the emperor's invitation? Like the laborer, we are shocked that the high and mighty reaches out to the poor and lowly. But the real resistance goes deeper. It is fear of intimacy. Kierkegaard concludes, "In the face of it (the invitation) he cannot acquire frankheartedness, and therefore must have it done away with, brought to naught and nonsense, for it is as though it would stifle him."

Intimate relationships challenge the autonomy we believe we possess. Most of us see ourselves as day laborers in the midst of emperors. Our self-esteem is low, so offers of caring make us uncomfortable. Why should they care for *us?* If we receive their care, what happens to our autonomy? Receiving makes us feel dependent: our fortress has been invaded.

Once I offered to do another person a favor. He obviously needed assistance, but he was reluctant to receive it. Though I finally convinced him to accept my offer, he was uncomfortable. I asked him why. "I just don't like to receive," he said.

Receiving is harder for many people than giving. As long as we are giving, we are "on top." The fortress is still intact. But when we receive we have to open up, we invite invasion. We feel obligated to justify receiving, to deserve it, even to reciprocate. We are no longer autonomous, no longer untouched. Yet if we want out of the fortress, which is our prison, this is the way, uncomfortable though it is.

Intimacy within Marriage

People fear intimacy even within the most intimate of relationships, marriage. Many images of marital intimacy are retained in our wedding rites. But it is one thing to get married and another to become married. The former takes a few moments, while the latter takes a lifetime. In reality marriage is an attitude as well as a state. A person living with another can be closed to intimacy even as a person living alone can be open to it.

During the early weeks of my own marriage, I found it a release from tension as well as a source of humor on occasion to shout, "I don't want to be a husband!" The occasion was usually some frustration over my new responsibilities—like a smoking furnace or a paycheck that did not fulfill our needs. There was probably as much truth as jest in those outbursts. Being married was demanding of me more than I was capable of or willing to give. I was not really ready to become married.

I was not unique in this respect. Many people who enter into marriage do not seem ready. Divorce has become an accepted escape from marriage frustrations, and increasing numbers are opting for it. The ancient vows are too demanding for modern people. "Until death do us part" seems unrealistic.

Alvin Toffler in *Future Shock* sees marriage as a lifelong union becoming obsolete. In its place he envisions "serial marriage." People will have one mate during youth, another for mid-life, and perhaps another for later years. The rationale is that medical science has made it possible for us to live longer, and it is unreasonable to commit oneself to stay married 50 years to the same person.

Yet we have had older people and 50-year marriages for a long time. I recall the golden wedding anniversaries of both my parents and my grandparents. Long-married people provide some of the strongest testimonies to the value of marriage. A recent study conducted among 50 couples who were married 50 years or more revealed that they were optimistic people who believed in marriage as a way of life and still enjoyed each other's company more than that of anybody else.[3]

Those who go from one marriage to another may never know the marital intimacy of these older couples. They encounter similar obstacles in each marriage but do not have the stick-to-it-tiveness to work through them. People can remain married without being intimate, but if they open themselves to intimacy, the years contribute to the growth of their relationship.

The sexual expression of this relationship joins the bodies of two people in a symbol of their union. According to St. Paul, their bodies do more than unite for an ecstatic experience. Through mutual commitment, their bodies are actually shared. Evidently some couples in his Corinthian congregation were withholding their bodies. "The husband," Paul wrote, "should give to his wife her conjugal rights, and likewise the wife to her husband." His rationale for this counsel was that in marriage their bodies belong to each other. "For the wife does not rule over her body, but the husband does; likewise the husband does not rule over his own body, but the wife does" (1 Cor. 7:3-4). Those whose bodies have become symbolic fortresses to protect their autonomy find such commitment to intimacy threatening.

Paul's words are in harmony with his own Hebrew tradition. In the Book of Genesis, husband and wife are depicted as leaving their parental homes to form a new unit of life described as "one flesh." The logical implication of these words, according to Jesus, is that this union is for life. "What God has joined together, let not man put asunder."

The Option of Interdependence

In our day many view commitment to marriage as curtailment of individual independence. Formerly this attitude was associated with men. A husband would refer to his wife as his ball-and-chain and say he preferred the company of "the boys." Today the resistance is coming from women. In their fight for equality, some feminists have attacked the marital state for restricting women's identity. Marriage to them means dependency, and they join their male counterparts of a previous age in extolling their independence.

They have a point. I recall the bitter clash I witnessed between a young husband and wife over the wife's supposed infidelity. It was August and the temperature in their upstairs apartment must have been close to 100 degrees. Their two small children were wearing next to nothing in an attempt to tolerate the heat. I do not know whether the wife was guilty, but if she was I could understand. Her husband expected her to be content taking care of the children in that cramped apartment day after day. She had little if any diversion. "You're getting three square meals a day," he yelled. "What else could you want!"

One can understand how this woman would long for liberation. Since her marital dependency symbolized bondage, liberation to her mind would be independence. Yet the other alternative, understandably overlooked, is interdependence.

To put forth this alternative, Nena and George O'Neill wrote their best seller, *Open Marriage*. According to the O'Neills, closed marriage is characterized by dependency and bondage. Since this form of marriage is no longer viable in our liberated age, the O'Neills present the option of open marriage as a way to save the institution. Open marriage permits mates to have a life outside of as well as within their marriage.

The only thing new about open marriage is the name. Although the O'Neills give the impression that open marriages were rare in previous generations, the qualities associated with openness—trust, flexibility in roles, honest communication—have characterized good marriages for a long time. The difference in our day is that closed marriages are less likely to be tolerated.

Belonging to another is not the same as being possessed by another. Belonging inspires trust while possessing leads to jealousy. Although my choice of words to denote this difference may be arbitrary, the difference in attitude toward oneself and toward others is very real. If persons are able to join with each other they are open to intimacy, and if they remain open their relationship will be a stimulus to their growth. If on the other hand they fear intimacy, they will need to possess each other, and the relationship they establish will stifle their growth. Each mate will feel stress as they chafe under their marital restrictions. Soon hostility will replace whatever positive attraction each may have held for the other.

Friendships as well as marriages can go sour on this note. Commitment may not be as total in friendship as in marriage, but there is similar potential for belonging. Some people need to possess their friends. They cannot tolerate flexibility in a relationship; to possess means to control. Since few people can tolerate being controlled for very long, such a friendship is destined to unresolvable conflict. It becomes a source of pain for both parties, and it soon cools and ultimately dies.

Sexual Union

Tension between belonging to another and yet retaining one's identity is symbolized in sexual intimacy. Although the symbol is one of union—the man entering into the woman's body and the woman opening to receive him—the culmination of this union is the highly self-oriented experience of orgasm. Masturbation is appealing precisely because orgasm is self-oriented: one can achieve the experience without the frustrations of relating to another person. We can fantasize another to accompany masturbation. Fantasy figures are completely under our control. We possess them absolutely.

Men and women can maintain isolation even during intercourse, in what appears to be intense intimacy. In spite of labels we attach to intercourse—be intimate, make love, come together—the act itself may be quite the opposite. Sex may be exploited to achieve selfish satisfaction. Then it is a substitute for intimacy rather than its expression. This is one reason that, in the midst of our so-called sexual liberation, we still lack intimacy. The increase in sexual activity has not diminished the problem of loneliness. In fact, it may well have intensified it.

As a corrective to this sorry situation, some people conceive of their role in sexual intercourse as primarily that of giver. We cannot correct one extreme by going to its opposite. Those who get involved primarily to give, like those concerned primarily with getting, are using the other person rather than relating to him or her. In their extremes they bypass the intimacy of interdependence. Our own needs are important, but so are the needs of the other. Behind sharing is caring.

I have used marriage as an illustration for all close relationships because the investment people make in their marriage magnifies what goes on in any personal relationship. Our potential for intimacy depends on our self-image and self-acceptance. The basic intimacy is intimacy with oneself. Intimacy means exposure. When we lack self-acceptance we protect ourselves from exposure either by withdrawing from others or by attempting to possess them. We can achieve self-acceptance through creative solitude.

CHAPTER 5

CREATIVE SOLITUDE:

How to Be Alone and Enjoy Yourself

You may wonder, When is this book going to get to the question of what we can *do* about our loneliness? The answer is *now*. It is necessary to understand any problem before we can talk about solutions to it. In fact, solutions grow out of such understanding. A problem as complex as loneliness is no exception. In the preceding chapters we have looked into this complexity. We are ready now to enter the problem-solving stage. We begin at the point to which our examination of the problem led us: our relationship with ourselves.

How do you feel about being confined for an evening to your own company? Many people spend time alone only when all efforts to have it otherwise have been frustrated. If the hours you spend with yourself are not particularly rewarding, you have a common problem. This fact is more out in the open today than in our more guarded past. Perhaps you see yourself as a loner. Being a loner, however, does not necessarily mean you enjoy your own company, any more than being with others necessarily means enjoying their company. If you feel you are stuck with yourself, you've yet to learn that solitude brings great potential for fulfillment.

Western civilization militates against solitude. We are oriented toward production, toward the practical. Creative solitude is a luxury we think we cannot afford. It would put us behind in our schedules. It might even undermine our interest in maintaining our schedules.

In *Sickness unto Death,* Soren Kierkegaard twitted the people of his day for their fear of being alone. "In the constant sociality of our age people shudder at solitude to such a degree that they know no other use to put it to but (Oh, admirable epigram!) as a punishment for criminals." Rather than being shackled to ourselves in solitary confinement, through creative solitude we find solitary expansion. We expand in our awareness of all that is going on within and outside of us.

Current Movements in Meditation

Jesus belongs to all time, all humanity. As a person in a particular time and place, however, he belonged to the East. The separation of East from West has been impoverishing to both. Now once again these worlds are meeting. Ironically, the invasion of Eastern religious practices into Western civilization is helping us appreciate more fully the humanity of Jesus.

In your wildest imagination, would you have envisioned 20 years ago, or even 10 years ago, that meditation would become an American fad? Certainly not in gregarious, outgoing, pragmatic America! Yet a phenomenal number of people of all ages, and particularly the young, are turning to transcendental meditation (TM) as a way of creative solitude. Even more amazing, the person most responsible for this phenomenon is an unpretentious guru from India. If we add to transcendantal meditators the large numbers involved in the related practice of yoga and the Buddhist-oriented exercises of Zen, we perceive not simply a fad but a trend. Americans are turning to the East to learn how to use their solitude creatively.

In Eastern forms of meditation, one focuses on something concrete to facilitate entry into a deeper level of consciousness. In transcendental meditation this is called the fourth level of consciousness—beyond waking, sleeping, and dreaming. TM uses the *mantra*—a word with no meaning provided to the meditator by the teacher—as a sound on which to focus. A Zen meditator focuses on a bodily function such as breathing or on a specific area of the body such as the abdomen. These are all means to assist meditators in listening to their own bodies, their own feelings, their own spirits, their own innermost yearnings.

This approach to solitude is entirely different from adjusting to being alone as the lesser of two evils. Some persons feel safer—even though miserable—in their own company, where they need not risk the pain of rejection. This kind of aloneness is not creative solitude; it is boredom. The large number of people participating in solitary meditation demonstrates that it is possible to enjoy one's own company. We can be alone and not experience loneliness. The hoped-for result of meditative practices is peace of soul, not pain. Yet even pain is accepted as grist for the meditative mill.

Directing a lonely person to concentrate on his relationship to himself may seem misguided. You may be sick of your company and want nothing more than to escape it. You desire the company of others. If it were a question of either your own company or the company of others, your misgivings would be justified. Fortunately we are not confronted with this choice. The way to relationships with others, paradoxically, is through getting in touch with your own being.

So let us begin our solution to the problem of loneliness with the cultivation of creative solitude. Risk being alone with yourself as a venture in discovery. Getting in touch with ourselves gets us in touch not only with our own humanity but with *all* humanity. Our pains are also others' pains; our pleasures are also their pleasures. Creative solitude is actually a base for community because it is the basis for our identity with humanity. We take our creative solitude with us into the world. It stays with us in the midst of people. Creative solitude establishes our identity and is the means for establishing relationships with others.

In *Reaching Out,* Henri Nouwen puts it well: "The movement from loneliness to solitude . . . creates the inner space where a compassionate solidarity with our fellow human beings becomes possible."

The Frontier Within

When we're alone, even if we're lonely, we are not without a relationship. The self is by definition a relationship —the relationship of *I* to *me.* This is why we can refer to our deceiving ourselves, punishing ourselves, forgiving ourselves, or being good to ourselves. *I* as a subject am aware of *myself* as object. This relation makes possible creative solitude. We can grow to enjoy our own company.

50

Memory and imagination play a large role in how we relate to ourselves. Our memory joins us to our past. It constitutes our awareness of ourselves as historical persons. Our imagination joins us to the future. Besides being persons who have been, we are also persons who are becoming. These connections with the past and the future give to the present moment—the moment of existence—both continuity and movement. They provide a base for reflection in creative solitude.

Henry David Thoreau went deeply into himself in search of his identity. Though he lived during a time of expanding geographical frontiers, the inner life was for him the most exciting frontier of all: "It is not worth the while to go around the world to count the cats in Zanzibar. Be a Columbus to whole new continents and worlds within you; opening new channels, not of trade but of thought." Today he would probably put his thoughts in space imagery: Be a John Glenn to whole new galaxies and universes within you.

Like explorations of new worlds and infinite space, exploration of the worlds within is more than a lark. The Columbuses and Glenns undergo rigorous training, and the explorations they undertake expose them to pain as well as pleasure. Not everything we see within us is attractive. Some of it may be repugnant—even frightening. We may want to look away and repress the memory.

The Solitary Quest

Our daughter's sudden death occurred just as my wife and I had completed our school year, with the summer before us and no teaching assignments. Some may have thought this the worst of all possible times. If we had to work we would have had something to occupy our time and minds. We did not see it this way. We were grateful for three months free of other demands so we could concentrate on our grief. Grieving is a very lonely and painful process. Although it helps to share grief with others, one also needs to grieve alone. Though our solitude that summer was painful, it was also creative. It helped us work through our grief to the point where we felt able to go on living.

People noted for creative use of solitude have knowingly put themselves into solitary situations from which it was difficult to escape. Thoreau, for example, cut off most of his contacts with society to live alone on Walden Pond for two years as an experiment in self-reliance. Among some Indian tribes, fathers traditionally sent each son alone into the forest when he reached a certain age to live on his own in preparation for manhood. In the forest he learned not only how to survive in the environment but also how to live with himself. If the ordeal proved too much and he returned before the stated time, he was humiliated before his people and not permitted to become a warrior.

We note a similar preparatory pattern for leadership in the Judeo-Christian tradition. After his leadership aspirations were deflated by his people's rejection, Moses fled to the land of Midian where he became a shepherd. Alone with his flocks in the wilderness, he saw the burning bush and heard the voice directing him to return to Egypt to liberate his people.

The solitude of the wilderness was familiar habitat for the prophets. Elijah received God's message in lonely places from which he emerged from time to time to deliver his oracles. This same pattern characterized the prophetic career of John the Baptist, the New Testament Elijah. He lived in the desert on locusts and wild honey and identified his calling with the words of the prophet Isaiah: "the voice of one crying in the wilderness."

Though his style of living contrasted with that of his cousin John, Jesus began his vocation in creative solitude. Led by the Spirit into the wilderness, he fasted 40 days, then emerged victorious over temptations of the devil. In this preparatory ordeal, he established his identity as God's Messiah. His response to his final temptation gave direction to his life: "You shall worship the Lord your God and him only shall you serve."

Cutting Off Escape Routes

Nouwen says, "In solitude we can become present to ourselves." It is not easy to "become present" to yourself, and if a way of escape is available, you may take it. This is why those who set about deliberately to become present to themselves cut off all possible escapes. They enter into their desert, their wilderness, their lonely place with a determination to stay there for the prescribed time.

Such disciplinary measures seem necessary if our solitude is to be used creatively. You have an inherent need to get in touch with the person inside. To meet this need you may have to put away all distractions for a time, reducing the press of external demands for your attention. Then focus with as little interruption as possible on the relationship between *I* and *me*.

The world of nature is the most desired milieu to encourage creative solitude. Even after his 40 days alone in the wilderness, Jesus repeatedly withdrew to the mountains or the deserts or the gardens for quiet time alone or with his disciples. The awesome beauty of nature stimulates our sense of kinship with all of creation. Aesthetic appreciation of beauty and quiet is pleasant to both body and soul. Natural surroundings symbolize inner peace and tranquility. They assist us in getting in step with the rhythm of creation—with our own rhythm.

CHAPTER 6

INTIMACY WITH NATURE:

Relating to Other Forms of Life

The choice of nature as a setting is conducive to relating to oneself not simply because of its aesthetic appeal. We have a kinship with nature: we belong to it, are part of it, and can relate to it. Communing with nature is no mere figure of speech. We have an affinity even for the inanimate parts of nature. The stars and planets have always fascinated us, and the ancient study of astrology is based on the belief that these bodies influence our lives. The mountains and seas have similar appeal. I have a friend who has a love affair with the ocean. It is more to him than a place in which to sail and scuba dive. It is an extension of himself.

Our Kinship with Nature

We are attracted to nature because we have a common Creator. Our origin is in nature, for God created us out of the dust. Our destiny is also in nature, for to dust we shall return. Out of this identity we relate to the sea and the stars. Our bodies and spirits were meant to join harmoniously in rhythm with the rest of creation.

As a gardener I share with others the love for plants. I know all my plants individually. I become enthusiastic over watching them grow. I awaken excited to see what has happened during the night. Plants do better, it is said, when they are loved and even talked to. Experiments have demonstrated such claims may have some validity. Are plants actually capable of responding to a person? There is some reason to believe they are.

Our kinship with animals is even stronger than our affection for plants. My friend who loves the ocean also loves to watch whales. He shares Captain Ahab's fascination, but in a positive way. He watches whales as though keeping an appointment with them. I also know a young woman who likes to get away from her city job to ride alone on her horse. In riding she joins herself to the animal's greater power, and she controls that power. But she also cares for her horse and enjoys being with him.

Nature provides us with good company. The horse, the dog, and the cat receive affection and return it. Older people who suffer loneliness and isolation can be comforted by the presence of a pet. An animal is a far better companion than the illusory person on the television screen or the illusory warmth of the bottle.

Among contemporary writers, John Steinbeck stands out for his awareness of our kinship with nature. His stories contain vivid descriptions of natural phenomena and in particular of our relationship to animals. *The Red Pony,* for example, is a touching story of a boy's love for his pony and of the crisis in his life when the pony becomes ill and finally dies. *Of Mice and Men* contains a moving account of a similar relationship between a pathetic old ranch hand and his equally pathetic old dog. Here also is a tragic dimension. An unsympathetic bunk mate callously puts the dog "out of its misery," leaving the old fellow in his own misery for not undertaking the distasteful task himself. Steinbeck describes his own relationship to nature in *Travels with Charley,* the story of his journeys through America accompanied by his dog.

Among earlier American writers sensitive to nature, Thoreau is preeminent. At Walden Pond he was preoccupied with relating to his immediate environment. He described the pond as his "great bedfellow," and in spring when it made loud noises as it thawed, he referred to it as "flatulating." His daily alarm clock was a red squirrel who scampered onto his roof in the morning "as if sent out of the woods for this purpose." He observed the ants in battle and listened to the loon and the ducks as kindred spirits.

While living with nature is not a substitute for living with people, it can improve our human relations. Such was the case with Thoreau. In contrast to his years prior to Walden, those following are described by Brooks Atkinson as "conspicuously social."

A People Identified with Nature

American Indians are a people known for close identification with nature. Festive ceremonies and ritual traditions of the various tribes are oriented to nature and natural phenomena. Indian names—Sitting Bull, Black Elk, Little Crow, Black Hawk—indicate how they saw themselves as part of nature. In contrast to whites, who often exploited and laid waste the natural environment,

Indians used only what they needed. While whites slaughtered whole herds of buffalo, often just for their hides, Indians killed only enough for an adequate food supply. It is no wonder modern Indian leaders are concerned about preserving their native culture, which is being undermined by the apathy of poverty and the ever-eroding influence of white "civilization."

Sensitivity to the natural environment provided native Americans with wisdom that industrialized nations sorely lack. Living in close dependence on the natural environment, Indians were aware they shared life and death with all creatures. Since death occurred naturally in the life about them, they perceived it as a natural also for them. In *I Heard the Owl Call My Name,* Margaret Craven's powerful novel, a young Anglican clergyman learns to accept his own imminent death by living with the Kwakiutl Indians in British Columbia. His bishop assigns him to this parish rather than informing him of his terminal illness, hoping the young man will be better prepared when he has to learn the truth. Ostensibly the clergyman is sent to minister to the Indians; in reality they were also to minister to him.

In his short time with these people, the young clergyman learns to love them and to appreciate the wisdom they've accumulated through close identification with the woods and the sea. They believe that when a person hears the owl call his name, his death is imminent. When the clergyman becomes increasingly aware that his health is dissipating, he hears the owl call his name.

Realizing he has only a short time to live, his most difficult task is leaving the Indians to return to the other world—the world of agonizing loneliness—to die. Then the people offer him their "unexpected gift of peace"—

the invitation to stay, to die, with them. Here he could die because here he had *lived*.

Nature as a Medium of Revelation

The Judeo-Christian heritage in which most of us have been reared has not entailed close identity with nature. Emphasis rather has been on the difference between humans and other forms of life: humans alone were created in God's image, and they were to have dominion over other forms of life, to fill the earth with their progeny and subdue it.

In the end nonhuman forms of life fail to satisfy our need for intimacy. Adam could give names to all the plants and animals, but he could not find among them a helper fit for him. Because of Adam's loneliness, God caused a deep sleep to fall on him, and from Adam's own rib God made a woman and brought her to Adam. Adam's response expressed his feelings. "This at last is bone of my bones and flesh of my flesh" (Gen. 2:23).

Nature, however, does play a mediating role in the old covenant. When Job's sufferings led him into extreme loneliness, he was restored to intimacy with himself and God through contemplation of nature. His fourth comforter, Elihu, directed Job's attention to the marvels of creation to jar him loose from his narrow focus on self-pity. "Hear this, O Job; stop and consider the wondrous works of God. Do you know how God . . . causes the lightning of his cloud to shine? . . . Can you, like him, spread out the skies, hard as a molten mirror?" (Job 37: 14-18). When God enters the conversation, he too asks Job to contemplate the marvels of nature. "Have you entered into the springs of the sea, or . . . the storehouses of the snow? . . . Can you bind the chains of the Pleiades, or loose the cords of Orion? . . . Do you know when the mountain goats bring forth? . . . Who has let the wild ass go free? . . . Do you give the horse his might? . . . Is it by your wisdom that the hawk soars?" (from Job 38–41).

The procedure worked. By turning his attention from his own misery to the marvels of nature, Job's mind became open to the Spirit of God. Through contemplating the fascinating variety within creation, he became reconciled to the Creator and received peace.

A Christian known for his communication with nature is St. Francis of Assisi. Following in the way of Jesus, who retreated to the mountains, deserts, and gardens for prayer and used the lilies, trees, and sparrows for illustrations, Francis could literally not see the forest for the trees. Each tree was for him unique, a story in itself. Each flower and animal was a child of God and therefore a brother or sister to Francis. In "Canticle of the Sun," he calls even the inanimate parts of nature brother sun, sister moon, brother wind, sister water, and brother fire. Earth is mother earth and death is sister death. His intuitive ability to communicate with animals led to amazing feats, such as taming a wolf and converting doves into pets. Such stories seem legendary, but they cannot be discounted as beyond possibility. Francis had this same power in his relationships to people, whom he saw as unique individuals. Every form of life was his intimate kin.

Because he was in harmony with all of life, Francis has been called the patron saint of ecologists. His belief in the equality of all creatures is an alternative in Christendom to the idea of human dominance in subduing nature. Obviously modern technology rejected this alternative.

Yet the two positions need not be opposites. "Subdue" does not mean despoil. Thoreau, like the American Indians, hunted animals for food—a way of subduing nature. But he and they followed nature's own laws for survival, taking only what they needed. They did not try to possess nature.

Even those who prefer to emphasize human dominion over nature need to remember that this dominion is under God. It is his world, not ours. We are managers responsible to him. As the hymn puts it:

> This is my Father's world,
> And to my listening ears
> All nature sings, and round me rings
> The music of the spheres.
> This is my Father's world;
> I rest me in the thought
> Of rocks and trees, of skies and seas,
> His hand the wonders wrought.

The Wider Context of Belonging

My purpose in this chapter has been to provide the experience of belonging with a context wider than the human scene. People are not off by themselves, separate from the rest of creation. They are a part of nature, and all of creation is the context for human living. Estrangement from the rest of creation has brought loneliness. Through possessive attempts to subdue nature, we have become estranged from it. As a consequence we become estranged also from our own *human* nature.

The nostalgic return of some people to primitive ways of living is no coincidence. They are trying to recover their natural context. Industrial society is in danger of destroying that context. With the pollution of our air, water, and soil, we are threatening our own existence. Our loneliness is a symptom of estrangement from our natural habitat.

To cope positively with loneliness, we need to see ourselves as part of a larger context—the context of creation. We can begin with our bodies, since our estrangement from nature begins with estrangement from our *physical* nature. Enjoying our bodies is a vital step in learning to relate to nature, for it is with our physical senses that we perceive the physical world about us.

CHAPTER 7

THE INNER DIALOG:

Relating to God

We began our approach to a solution to loneliness with learning to relate to ourselves, because this particular relationship is the easiest to avoid. Being present to ourselves can be painful, and reaching out to other people can be merely an attempt to escape from that pain. Much socializing is of this nature and therefore is superficial.

Usually we do not feel quite so lonely when we are with convivial people, but loneliness remains a constant threat. The desperate need to be with people to counteract the pain of loneliness may even increase our fear of being alone. Superficial socializing may be an obstacle to coming to grips with loneliness, rather than a solution. We are still lonely, even when with people. Socializing is only a temporary distraction, unless we have inner peace.

The Outstretched Arms of God

Soren Kierkegaard understood how to solve problems through the inward route. He was a psychologist before Wundt and an analyst before Freud. He went into himself as few others have through a process he called reflection. Reflection is opposite from a state of immediacy in which one is in constant interaction with one's environment—other people or things—as a distraction from looking into oneself.

But Kierkegaard also discovered limits to reflection. The more he got into himself, the more distress he experienced. He called his distress *sickness unto death* or *despair*. He found that the only constructive way out of despair is the leap of faith into the outstretched arms of God.

When we move into ourselves, we must also move in the direction of God. Others have described the inward journey in this way. William James, pioneer in the psychological study of religious experience, referred to an inner door of consciousness leading to the world of the Spirit, in contrast to an outer door leading to the external environment.

Contemporary psychologist-physician Paul Tournier takes a dim view of introspection as a means to genuine confrontation with the self. He describes this internal entry of the world of the Spirit as the *inner dialog*. He believes the journey inward becomes valuable only when introspection is converted into a relationship with the Spirit of God. Relating to oneself, therefore, embraces more than dialog between *I* and *me;* it is also a dialog between one's spirit and the Spirit of God—an encounter described by St. Paul as the Spirit's *bearing witness* with our spirit.

As noted in Job's contemplation of nature, our relationship with creation also culminates in the Spirit. The movement from relating to creation to relating to the Creator is familiar to many cultures and ages. The New

Testament goes beyond this general revelation through nature to a specific revelation through *human* nature in the person of Jesus, who in effect is the outstretched arms of God to which Kierkegaard testified.

The Loneliness of Guilt

The way to God through the inner door of consciousness has its obstacles. Many of us know from experience the pain Kierkegaard encountered in his reflections. It is no wonder we try to distract our attention from ourselves by socializing or by other interactions with our environment. As one of my students put it, "How can you look within yourself when you don't like yourself?"

What we feel when we look within is guilt, though today we label it inferiority complex or low self-image. When we feel guilty we are aware of our uniqueness in a very negative way. Shame overcomes us when we fail. Shame not only isolates us from others but makes us painfully aware of our isolation.

We are also frightened—particularly of the power we believe we possess to hurt and destroy others, especially those we love. We beat on ourselves for being so cruel, so insensitive, so stupid, so inadequate. Our sense of unworthiness blocks us from genuine contact with others. No loneliness exceeds the loneliness that grows out of guilt.

In such loneliness, the outstretched arms of Jesus extend to us God's forgiveness, his acceptance of us as we are. The arms are not seen by our eyes. They are extended through the inner door of consciousness where they are perceived by the eye of faith. The leap of faith toward these arms is the leap from the loneliness of guilt to communion with God, from inner loneliness to inner dialog.

Communication with God

Communion with God takes place through prayer. The usual image we have of praying is a person with the head bowed, perhaps on bended knees, expressing needs and concerns to God in silence. Actually prayer is more a way of life than a distinct activity, even as friendship is more the awareness in memory or in reality of a comfortable presence than of specific conversations.

While presence is comforting, absence is not. The problem with prayer is what Henri Nouwen describes as the problem of God's absence. Faith implies doubt, and sometimes doubt seems stronger than faith. Those outstretched arms of God: are they really there? No wonder a leap is necessary if we are to believe—a leap over the obstacle of doubts.

Doubts are always with us; they go with faith. At times, however, they seem to block out faith. Perhaps you know such times from personal experience; perhaps you are in such a time now. In my bereavement I asked God, often out loud as though attempting to reach him, "Where are you!" He was hidden by the tragedy of my daughter's death, yet by faith I knew he was present.

Although he was the revelation of God to humans, Jesus also experienced the absence of God. In anguish on the cross he cried out, "My God, my God, why hast thou forsaken me?" Yet he took the leap of faith by commending his spirit into God's hands as he died.

If you are in a period of doubting, take that leap yourself. Commit yourself—in spite of the problem of God's

66

absence—to faith in his presence. The satisfactions that follow, however sporadically, are reassuring. Through the inner dialog that accompanies faith, you will have a relationship of intimacy even when you are alone.

There is a constancy in the reality of God's presence. I find great satisfaction in knowing I can pause any time to listen to his Spirit. When I am serious about listening, he speaks clearly. I receive power for self-direction by envisioning the outstretched arms of Jesus beckoning me to surrender, to give up distressing thoughts and feelings and to accept in their stead the peace of soul that comes from his reconciling love.

Security through Faith

The inner dialog provides a sense of belonging; we know who we are by knowing whose we are. The inner dialog also helps us feel secure—a decided asset in engaging in outer dialogs. By confronting our loneliness at its source in our inner self, our relationship with God provides us with an internal intimacy as a basis for establishing intimate relationships with others.

By focusing on our relationship to God apart from our relationships to people, it may seem that these are separate and that our relationship with God is established prior to our relationships to people. This is not correct. While we can and must distinguish our relationship with God from our relationships with people, we cannot separate them.

The first relationship we experience is with our mother or mothering person in infancy. However, this relationship communicates God's love as well as the mother's love. Parents and God are not as distinguished in children's minds as they are in the minds of adults. As children's individuality grows, however, the situation changes. They become aware of their aloneness—that they are separated from others—and develop their own "space."

In adolescence this space is often symbolized by the actual space of one's own room. Adolescents want the luxury of their own room if they can get it, and they would like not only brothers and sisters, but also parents, to stay out of their room unless given permission to enter. They no longer want to confide in parents regarding matters that belong to their space. If parents and God continue to blend together in the adolescent mind, God also is excluded. Aloneness then becomes loneliness.

During a class on loneliness, a woman told me her need for privacy existed as far back as she could remember. Even as a child of three she asked people to go away and leave her alone. In growing into adulthood she avoided people in any numbers, feeling tense and crowded when with them. The turning point in her life came when she began to believe in God. After that she no longer felt tense and threatened when she was with people. A relationship with God had entered her inner space, changing the nature of her privacy. She was secure enough in her own identity to enter rooms full of people in comfort.

Inner Marriage

Although it is mediated through parents and other people, our relationship with God is unlike our relationship with these people. The crucial difference is that God belongs in our inner space, while people are invited in on a selective basis and in ways limited by our need to be uniquely ourselves. The relationship that belongs in our space is defined in Old and New Testaments as marriage with God. This marriage was not simply between the individual and God, but between God and his people. In the Old Testament it is between Yahweh and the people of Israel; in the New Testament, between Christ and the church.

This corporate identity of the bride illustrates that our relationship with God is never separated from our relationship with people. The church is compared by St. Paul to a human body; church members are like members of an organic body that function together as parts of a whole. The members of the body of Christ relate to Christ as bodily organs relate to the head or brain. We have individual communication with Christ within the context of our relationship to the other members of the body. In communication with us as individuals, God "dwells in our hearts." His marital commitment is his bestowal of unconditional love, and our commitment is response to his love in the leap of faith. When we believe in God we are committed, married, to him in spirit, so that in the deepest recesses of aloneness we are open to his presence.

Not all of us marry or need to marry another person. Single people are whole persons complete in themselves. We can overcome the negative influences of our loneliness without becoming married. This is not true, however, in regard to spiritual marriage. All of us need to be married in spirit to be complete persons, secure enough in our inner balance to reach out to other persons. One of Ernest Becker's outstanding contributions in the Pulitzer Prize-winning book *Denial of Death* is his presentation of the insights of psychoanalyst Otto Rank, whose contribution to human wisdom has been largely obscured. A person, says Rank, is a "theological being," not a biological one.

It is inherent in human nature that we surrender to God, not out of weakness but as the fulfillment of our being—a fulfillment we need as a basis for social life. As Becker points out, Rank speaks not as a theologian but as a psychoanalyst, a scientist, and yet he agrees with Kierkegaard on the need for a religious solution to human loneliness.

Inner marriage completes—restores—our full humanity. The distinctive feature about the biblical description of humanity as created in God's image is that the image is *reflected*. It depends on God and his people being in communion. When the fall of humanity disrupted this communion, our potential for reflecting God's image was also disrupted. The spiritual marriage brought about by God's commitment of unconditional love through Jesus' mediation restored us again to intimacy, and as a consequence, to a reflection of God's image. It is an uneven reflection, however, because of our egocentricity.

We reflect the image of God when God is our center. The fall is a fall into off-centeredness. Inner marriage restores us to our center, our balance, bringing us into harmony with our own being. Once balanced, we can tolerate increasing self-awareness and consciousness expansion, though our dark side may be revealed. When we are united with God by his unconditional love, awareness of this dark side is less threatening. Our security permits us instead to utilize this awareness for personal growth.

Relating vs. Possessing

Our inward balance determines whether we relate to others or attempt instead to possess them. When we are unbalanced, we seek to find our center in a particular person or group. We experience others not so much as persons to be known but as persons who can meet our needs. This is an expectation they cannot fulfill because in reality we are asking—demanding—that they play God. Even if they were willing to entertain this illusion—and some people seem to enjoy it at least for a time—they cannot.

Romanticism fosters the illusion that we can find fulfillment through a lover. George made this mistake. He was very lonely and longed for a romanticized lover who would take his loneliness away. He found her—several times. At the beginning of each relationship to the woman of his dreams, George entered "the third heaven," but each time his romantic illusions were inevitably destroyed.

As a relationship progressed, he began to demand more and more from his lover. His desire proved insatiable because he wanted her to fill his entire inner space. This was too much for her, and she began to back away. George reacted by being hurt. He depended on his romanticized image of the lover. He pleaded with her to fulfill his desires. His dependency was too big a burden; it frightened her away. "I can't be responsible for your happiness," she said.

Instead of realizing that she was facing reality, George became desperate and called her continuously. She finally severed the relationship entirely. George felt abused and sorry for himself, "Why does this always happen to me?" he asked. He was too preoccupied with his needs to see his complicity in dooming the relationship.

What happened to George in his love relationship applies equally to friendships with persons of either sex. Possessiveness and jealousy are not confined to man-woman relationships. The need for another person to fill our inner emptiness is the precursor of these destructive tendencies. People who need others to complete them are hypersensitive to "rivals." Realizing their inner poverty, they have little confidence in their own worth and feel inadequate to compete. Their energies go instead into jealousy and appeals for pity, which make them unattractive and only hasten the demise of the relationship. They live out their own self-fulfilling prophecies—they "knew it couldn't last."

In contrast, when our relationship with God occupies our inner space, the security coming from our dialog with him enables us to accept the natural limits to outer dialogs. Then our relationships with others are constructive.

CHAPTER **8**

COMMUNION WITH OTHERS:

Relating to People

Finally we are ready to discuss our relationships with other people. Though we are taking this subject up last, the implication is not that other people are incidental to easing loneliness. However, it is natural for a lonely person to assume that intimacy with another person is the sole solution to loneliness. Since the problem has much wider scope than this assumption would permit, so also does the solution. Though other people are not incidental to the solution, they are not the sole preoccupation of the solution process.

Relating to nature, to animals, to ourselves, and even to God does not eliminate our need for other persons. Nor is their significance for our relationship with other people one of sequence. Though I have chosen to discuss relationships to nature, animals, the self, and God in a sequential way, there is no sequential process involved. One relationship does not necessarily lead to another in terms of cause and effect. Instead, relationships may occur simultaneously. Relating to oneself, to nature, to animals, to God, and to other people are not only all equally important for the easing of loneliness, but they are also interdependent in this easing. Significant experience in any one of these areas enhances one's potential for significant experience in any of the others.

Our Need for Human Companions

In the downtown section of the city of Curitiba, Brazil, are huge statues of Adam and Eve in the nude. When the statues were first erected, citizens complained that such huge displays of nudity, even in stone, were offensive. Eve was removed and placed in the back garden of the governor's palace, leaving Adam alone in the public square. This arrangement seemed equally unsatisfactory. Finally the mayor decreed that Eve be replaced beside Adam. "It is not good," he said, quoting from Genesis, "that the man should be alone."

Although the mayor's quotation was in harmony with the context of the story of Adam and Eve, this early commentary on man's need for human companionship applies to more than his relationship to a woman. It describes human beings' communal nature. Some animals are loners. The tiger mates to procreate but otherwise prefers solitude. Others, such as the lion, form communities in their need for association. People are in this latter category. We need friends and intimates to fully experience living. Whether in nonindustrialized or modern societies, we are communal by nature. We gather together in tribes, communities, and cities, not only for protection and survival, but also for enjoyment.

Although I have chosen to discuss it last, relating to other persons is basic to all other relationships. Without relationships to other persons, human infants would probably not survive. Besides needing food, they need also to be held. Other forms of life mature whether their physiological needs are met by their own species or by some other, such as humans. But human infants need to be related to people to develop into human beings.

Wilderness Children

Children discovered in the wilds, where they lived without human company, behave more like animals than like human beings. The film *Wild Child* presents one prominent case of a boy found in a forest in France and a psychiatrist's effort to humanize him. After many frustrations, the psychiatrist's patience and ingenuity eventually triumphed as the child gradually began to make distinctly human responses.

In 1974 a child approximately eight years old was discovered in the African nation of Burundi. He had been living with monkeys in a jungle in which lost persons seldom survived. Evidently he had wandered into the jungle or was left there very early in his life. At this writing, after more than a year of training under a Russian psychiatrist, he still is more monkeylike than human. He walks on all fours, chatters, and jumps about like his fellow monkeys, and is stronger than a normal boy of his age. The hair on his body has disappeared since he was clothed. He is toilet trained and walks on two legs, but it is doubtful he will ever learn to talk, and his reactions when frightened are still monkeylike. A nurse associated

with his treatment raised the disturbing question of whether it would have been kinder to leave him with the monkeys where he felt he belonged.

Communal Religious Practices

Only through human associations can people develop
their potential to relate to nature, to themselves, and even
to God—as human beings. It is not coincidental that religious practices tend to be communal. Christianity in particular is oriented to human relationships, with its central
doctrine of the incarnation and with its focus on life in
congregations. God became *enfleshed* in a human being to
reveal himself to us. Jesus did not cease being human in
his personal union with the divine, nor was he less than
divine in his being fully human. This humanization of
God is reflected in the human fellowship of the church.
The New Testament even identifies the church as "Christ's
body."

Life with other people presents problems. In the early
days of Christianity, some reacted to these problems by
withdrawing into the desert to live as solitary Christians.
The most famous was Simeon Stylites who tried to separate himself even from the earth by positing himself on a
60-foot pillar where he lived for 30 years without ever
descending. But like many other desert hermits, he was
far from isolated. Disciples supplied him with food and
provided an audience for his preaching ministry.

While such solitary withdrawal occurred sporadically
until the sixteenth century, withdrawal was more often
to monasteries and nunneries, where organized communities of believers replaced the heterogeneous community
of society. Monks and nuns renounced their potential for

marriage and family, but the monastical community itself became their family, even to the vow of obedience to the abbot parent.

The social nature of Christianity is dramatized in the Sacrament of the Lord's Supper. By its very nature, the Lord's Supper is communal. When St. Paul warned the Corinthian congregation that, for genuine participation in the Sacrament, they needed to discern the Lord's body, he implied a two-fold understanding of this body. First is the body and blood of Christ, the elements of reconciliation, communicated through the bread and wine from the world of nature. In distributing the bread, Jesus said, "This is my body which is given for you." Second is the communing body, the body of Christ as the church. Through the members of this body, the head of the body —Christ—is revealed. Both bodies need to be discerned if one is to appreciate the full meaning of the Lord's Supper as Holy *Communion*.

It is not incidental that Holy Communion is a meal—a congregational, family meal. The family table is the focus of family living. A meal has a purpose beyond the necessary and enjoyable consumption of food. It is also a time of intimacy. A friend of mine fasts a day a week, but on this day he still sits with the family at the evening meal. Although he abstains from eating, he does not want to miss the experience of family intimacy.

When the family table succumbs to the pressures of business or favorite TV programs, these other supposed priorities do not compensate for the loss. People who live alone, particularly older people who have known the intimacy of the family table, may lose their incentive to prepare their meals. It is a time of pathetic contrast and their present loneliness deprives even their food of its appeal. The malnutrition that results is not only from a poverty in food but also from a poverty in intimacy. To meet their need for a balanced diet, the meals on wheels program has been developed by churches, hospitals, and other community organizations. But meals on wheels brings more than food to lonely older people—it brings also an accompanying human being who, though she may visit only briefly, slightly reconnects the tie between food and people. In his last year of living alone, my father would stand in his driveway a half hour before the arrival of meals on wheels, anticipating the contact—the only one he may have had the entire day.

Security through Physical Presence and Touch

The inner dialog with God and the outer dialog with people support each other. Ties of trust we develop with God and with other people diminish our suspicions and fears. Through these relationships, we develop a spirit of cooperation. This works as an antidote to the competitive spirit, inherent in our society, which moves us to hide our true identity from others as we exploit them to our own advantage.

The word *intimate* has taken on sexual connotations in our culture. For this reason the word is used to describe a relationship between the sexes. In the Bible the verb used to describe the sexual union of man and woman is *to know*. As a way of knowing another, this union is the symbol of *one flesh,* the biblical metaphor for the relationship created when a man and woman commit themselves to sharing life. Not only is this intimate relationship compared to that between God and his people, but the same word, *know,* is used to describe intimacy also with God.

The mutuality between the inner and outer dialogs is, of course, not limited to a specifically sexual understanding of intimacy. Sexuality itself is much broader than the specific expression of sexual intercourse. This broader understanding is revealed through the compassionate expression and the affectionate touch. The sexual dimension of intimacy centers in the tangible nature of the support we receive—of being held by another, whether literally or symbolically.

In the village of Vilcamba in southern Ecuador live the oldest people in the western hemisphere. A reporter who interviewed these centenarians found them refreshingly down to earth in their appreciation of life. An elderly woman talked with unabashed simplicity about the happiness that comes to a woman when she lies in the arms of the man she loves. Nothing in all her years, she said, had equalled that "quiet sense of joy and well-being." [4]

The security that comes through physical touch may account for the mystique associated with the nurse. In contrast to the physician, who is characterized more by a God-like distance, the closeness of the nurse is communicated not simply by her presence but by her touch. Gender is probably of little significance. As a hospital chaplain I saw male orderlies achieve similar intimacy with their patients. The isolation of the sick is penetrated in a sensory way when they experience the caring touch of one whose vocation is to help them.

Yet the mere *presence* of a caring person may symbolize intimacy. Living with another person may be of value in itself apart from any sexual connotation, broad or specific. Many women are rearing children alone. Sometimes a single man moves in with such a family as a convenience to both. A recent study of this unusual arrangement showed that usually the man and woman are not sexually involved although often a fatherly relationship exists between the man and the children.

The most familiar experiment in living together is the commune. Communes meet the immediate need of lonely people for the physical presence of others in a cooperative sharing of life. In recent history most communes came into being during the counterculture movement, and most of them no longer exist. Communes are often short-lived because intimacy—even when limited to the physical presence of cooperative workers—brings not only security, but also pain. Communes are no escape from the irritation and friction well known to college roommates and to biological families. Idealistic commune members are often disillusioned when they discover that the problems which made them disdain their own families reappear in the family of the commune. Discouraged, they may feel limited to a choice between living alone with the pain of isolation or living with others and experiencing a similar loneliness caused by conflict and hostility.

Coping with the Pain of Intimacy

Intimacy means exposure. To become close to another, you open yourself, share yourself, and this makes you vulnerable. You may be hurt—perhaps you have been. Perhaps the thought of being hurt again frightens you.

Fear of being hurt may prompt you to withdraw into your self-protecting shell, choosing loneliness because it seems less threatening than exposure. But by withdrawing, you trade an immediate six for a less immediate half dozen. This dilemma was well put by one caught in it:

"I'm so miserable without you, it is almost like having you around."

You need to weigh realistically the risk of pain brought by intimacy. In any intimate relationship you are wedded or joined to another. Some relationships, such as marriage, are less easily severed than others, but few are severed without some degree of pain.

Fear of intimacy involves fear of losing the apparent freedom of being unpledged, unattached. It also involves fear of losing your identity. The overture of sharing, of committing yourself to another, seems irretrievable.

These fears—as well as the irritations associated with intimacy—tend to increase when one is confined to a single or small number of significant relationships. *Open Marriage* is addressed to this situation. The O'Neills' thesis is that it is not good to confine one's intimate relationships to one's mate or other family members. The same could be said about limiting one's intimate friendships to one individual or to a very small circle. Restricting primary relationships to one or two puts too much pressure on these relationships to meet all of our intimacy needs. It also limits opportunities that come from knowing others. The O'Neills use the term *closed* to describe such restricted relationships. They strongly believe that such confinement is destructive to intimacy. They advise us to distribute our involvement among more people, to let our relationships be open to expanding interests and associations.

If you put all your intimacy eggs into one basket, dependency develops. The other person, whether friend or mate, exerts too much control over your life. By establishing other friendships, you gain other channels for your intimacy needs, in case any one relationship becomes temporarily troubled and its channel blocked. The O'Neills acknowledge the risk in this expansion of our intimate relationships, especially to marriage. Yet they believe that confinement of our intimacy needs to one person is a greater risk. They also believe the risk to marriage is considerably lessened if each mate has a separate identity that is not inextricably tied to the other.

Marriage Encounter

The O'Neills' stated goal is to save marriages, but I am not acquainted with any research concerning the results. Obviously many people are experiencing problems concerning intimacy. The O'Neills' book is a best seller, and their argument seems to make sense.

However, Catholic Marriage Encounter takes a different approach to intimacy. The movement has achieved such popularity that Lutheran Marriage Encounter, Episcopal Marriage Encounter, and Jewish Marriage Encounter have also been established, based on the same format. These movements center in a highly structured weekend retreat for married couples. A structure for daily marital dialog and a follow-up support group are organized. The emphasis is not on less togetherness, but on more, and on the interrelationship between one's marriage with God through his church and one's marriage with a mate. The O'Neills' model for marriage would approximate what Encounter calls "married singles."

My wife and I were impressed by the enthusiasm of couples who participated in Encounter, and now we have experienced this valuable weekend for ourselves. Many couples were present for the Encounter we attended, but the time apart from the formal presentations was spent almost entirely with one's spouse in the arduous discipline of marital dialog. The purpose of dialog is not to change one's mate or to defend oneself or even to solve problems in the relationship, but rather to express one's feelings and to listen to and accept the feelings of the other. In short, the purpose is to enhance the knowing, the intimacy of the relationship. The follow-up is a commitment to a 20-minute dialog period each day and regular meetings with a support group.

The result of Encounter for us and for many other couples we know is not the possessive spirit the O'Neills might anticipate, but rather openness of spirit. There is no chafing at restraints. Rather there is enjoyment of intimacy, growing mutuality of interests, and expanding knowledge of oneself and one's mate. The people involved are more open rather than less open with others, even those of the opposite sex. The reason is obvious: in such closeness of spirit there is no doubt about the other's loyalty. Instead there is trust—both of one's mate and of oneself.

The O'Neills give rules and principles for developing trust and intimacy, but Encounter provides a social experience which helps generate implementing power. The many friends gained at the follow-up support group cut deeply into the isolation of the nuclear family. Encounter couples become a kind of extended family.

Dialog can create or sustain intimacy in other relationships as well. For example, in the Catholic Encounter weekend, priests have dialogs with priests. And Parent Effectiveness Training follows the same listening-sharing format in establishing intimacy between parents and children.

Growth in intimacy of one relationship need not threaten other relationships. It is not as though we have only so much intimacy to distribute. Rather our capacity for intimacy increases as we develop its potential. The quantity depends on the quality. Intimacy develops when we express our own feelings and listen to others express their feelings, and when we accept our own feelings and the feelings of others. To know is to understand, and to understand is to accept, to forgive.

CHAPTER 9

Taking Risks to Meet Your Needs

How do you deal directly with your loneliness? We often know how others should solve their problems better than we know what *we* should do.

Mrs. Smith is lonely and admits it. A widow in her senior years, she has withdrawn into her small apartment. She rejects invitations of her fellow church members who offer to take her to church and community functions. We easily see what Mrs. Smith should do—but evidently it isn't so easy for her.

John also admits he is lonely. In his early 20s, John says despairingly that he has tried everything but cannot seem to develop lasting friendships. John consistently comes on too strong. He overwhelms people the first time he meets them, talking too much and listening too little. After a time they become weary of his chatter and his obvious attempts to impress them. We easily see what John should do—but evidently it isn't so easy for him.

Caring persons have talked to both Mrs. Smith and John about what they need to do, but it seems to go in one ear and out the other. It's easy for us to view the problem as something outside ourselves. We can be our own worst enemies as we erect obstacles to the satisfaction of our needs.

Facing Your Own Needs

Perhaps you are somewhat uncomfortable because efforts to help yourself seem selfish. One of my counselees felt this way. "It seems like I'm doing these things—even when they are helpful to others—really for myself. It makes me feel guilty, even hypocritical. I even feel uncomfortable when I pray for myself," he said, "particularly if I ask for something specific. It seems I'm being self-centered and I cannot imagine God approving of this."

Many people feel selfish doing things for their own sake because they put *I* and *others* in mutually exclusive categories. The second of the great commandments sets the issue straight. "You shall love your neighbor as yourself." Love for self does not oppose love for others—it serves as the model. Elton Trueblood applies this principle of the mutuality of our loves even to parenthood, which is usually associated with unselfish devotion. Says Trueblood: "The parent makes the mistake, frequently, of concentrating on the child, when he would help the child more if he would concentrate upon himself. The parent must guard, accordingly, against the danger of too much self-sacrifice. If the sacrifice is obvious it defeats its purpose. Much as we help those whom we love by performing services for them, we help them more by being composed and happy persons. More good is done in personal relations by the habit of happiness than by obvious deeds of kindness" *(The Recovery of Family Life,* Harper, pp. 93-94).

As Trueblood himself indicates, his point about parenthood applies to all personal relationships. When we care for ourselves we *are* caring for others, particularly those with whom we are closely associated: our family members, our friends, and even our fellow workers. When our personal needs are not being met, our dissatisfaction is communicated directly or indirectly to those about us. Depression and defeatism are as contagious as joy and hope.

If we do not make the effort to satisfy our needs directly, we are likely to do so indirectly and perhaps even unconsciously. When our conscience will not permit us to seek the satisfaction we desire because we would be acting selfishly, our needs will seek their satisfaction through activities of which the conscience approves such as service to others or crusading for justice or supporting a righteous cause. Were we consciously aware of grinding our own ax in these services and causes, the results would be more healthy. But when the guise is so complete that we ourselves are seemingly unaware of this mixture in our motives, these ventures in service take on a destructive bent which frequently ends in disillusion. Even then we feel compelled to explain this disillusion "unselfishly." It is other people who are at fault; they are either ungrateful or unscrupulous and we are simply the victims of these unfortunate circumstances. It is amazing how clearly we perceive our own sins when we see them in others while still not acknowledging them as our own.

Caring for others is important. But before we are in a

position really to care for others, we need to examine our own needs to see how they can be met.

Overcoming Dependence

Some persons are so reluctant to say what they want that they convince themselves and others that they have no desires. By their passivity they force others to make what should be mutual decisions. "You decide," they say. "Whatever you want to do is all right with me." Although such displacement of responsibility has the appearance of unselfishness, it is actually a controlling device. The other is coerced not only into making the decision but also into taking the responsibility for its consequences. Passive individuals protect themselves from accountability.

Dependent persons, besides being manipulative, are ultimately unattractive. What at first seems an agreeable disposition turns out to be the dead weight of no opinion. The lack of stimulating dialog ultimately saps vitality from the relationship. There are exceptions, of course. Some persons need to dominate or possess others as a way of bolstering their egos. The lopsided relationship they form with dependent persons may endure, but at the expense of genuine dialog.

Sometimes lonely people try to shape themselves into pleasing personalities so others will like them. This ultimately backfires. Recently our family moved during the middle of the school year. Our son was confronted, not only with a new high school where groups had already formed, but also with an apartment "neighborhood" where very little association takes place. The result was loneliness. Following are his own reflections on how he responded to these circumstances.

This year when our family took a sabbatical leave to San Diego I was confronted with having to make new friends. At first I was not too successful. I would ask myself what was wrong with me. I tried to shape myself into a form of person who might be acceptable to others my age. Finally—I don't know quite how—I learned that I must first be able to live with my own person or self and accept myself the way I am and present myself as me alone and not change to please other people. I found out that I have some very good qualities and that I don't need to change for others. After this making friends was easy, and I, interestingly enough, filled a quota similar to the number of friends I had back home.

Learning to Trust

The greatest risk is encountered when we reach out to other people, since their response is unpredictable. God, nature, even our own self await our involvement. God has promised through Christ, for example, "Him who comes to me I will not cast out" (John 6:37). In a sense other persons are waiting also, but approaching them is more precarious. They have the freedom to say yes or no. We count the cost beforehand: How much disappointment can I take?

Before we make an overture to another, we need to make an initial investment in trust. Trust is a pump-primer in establishing relationships. Invest in trust. Share with others, and listen as they share with you. Through sharing and accepting of feelings, ties are established.

Trust is much broader than having a positive attitude toward an encounter. The context for this and any similar trust is the belief that love and not indifference is at the heart of the universe. Our faith in God is essential to our faith in people.

But trust is not the same as gullibility or failure to face reality. When certain persons make it clear by what they say and do, or by what they do *not* say and do, that they are not particularly interested in our friendship, it is not necessarily an act of faith to persist in our overtures. We may simply be unwilling to accept reality, to accept limitations we do not like.

Bob was a college student who wanted to be included in a tightly knit group of students who lived in his dormitory. In obvious ways members of the group indicated disinterest in accepting Bob as anything more than a friendly fellow dorm resident. Bob persisted in his overtures and was just as persistently rebuffed. He was insensitive to communication, and he also had a problem in the way he evaluated others.

Influence of Social Status

Our selection process for making overtures to others may be an obstacle in itself. Often it is shaped by cultural values and priorities. Particular individuals, couples, families, or groups are deemed popular, and others desire to be identified with them. College students like Bob are not the only ones influenced by these values. The same hierarchy of social status exists among the faculty of his college, in the echelons of the business world, in societies of professional people, and even in the followship of some churches.

Not only are such cultural ratings arbitrary and their bases shallow, they are also obstructions to the development of intimate relationships. If we let people's ascribed status determine how we relate to them, we set up barriers to genuinely knowing them. Some associate with persons of high status to elevate their own status, while others are attracted to those low in the hierarchy because they like to feel superior. Burdened by low self-esteem, they feel more secure with those of lower rank.

Our first challenge in improving our relationships with others is to free ourselves from the evaluation ratings of our culture. The goal is to perceive the worth of each individual in his or her own person, rather than in the advantages he or she offers to our ego. Jesus was as direct with Nicodemus, a man of high social status, as with the social outcast, Mary Magdalene. He looked neither up nor down in his observation of others, but straight ahead. Both the rich man, Joseph of Arimathea, and the poor women from Galilee were concerned with preparing his body for burial. Paul also ignored social distinctions. He referred to the original disciples of Jesus around whom a specific status was accruing as those "who were reputed to be something." But his own attitude was clear: "What they were makes no difference to me: God shows no partiality" (Gal. 2:6).

In a Christian perspective there is no social hierarchy, but only a mutual subjection one to another out of reverence for Christ (Eph. 5:21). All are peers. If we use the superficial rating scales of our culture to evaluate others, according to the epistle of James we have "become judges with evil thoughts" (James 2:4). The response of the Christian to all such social discrimination, James says, is to "show no partiality."

Because of the arbitrary way in which our society evaluates people, it overlooks jewels. This is a judgment on society rather than on the people overlooked. You may be one of the jewels. You may find others. You can begin by taking off the glasses of cultural evaluation so your eyes are emancipated to see people directly, as they are.

Beginning Today

Perhaps you are overwhelmed by the scope of the problem of loneliness. Any beginning point may seem so far removed from a solution that you lose incentive. But you have to begin somewhere, at some present moment—with the small effort that can be made today.

In describing the enormous odds facing people in countries resisting Nazi tyranny and the amazing exploits their resistance accomplished, William Stringfellow, in *An Ethic for Christians and Other Aliens in a Strange Land,* maintains that a major factor in these accomplishments was that the resisters were willing to do small, apparently insignificant tasks that could be done *today.* "Each one of these if regarded in itself seems far too weak, too temporary, too symbolic, too haphazard, too meek, too trivial to be efficacious against the aggressive, monolithic pervasive presence of Nazism." But they were effective. So don't be concerned if what you can do *now* to improve your situation seems insignificant. It's the consistent, accumulative effect that counts—once you begin.

First ask yourself: What is the quality of my relationship to myself, to nature, to other persons, and—"in, with, and under" and beyond these—to God? Where do I need to improve? Where might I focus as my growing edge?

Decide where you should begin on the basis of your circumstances, your insights, and your desires. Then plan a program for action, and act on that program. Our purpose in coming to grips with our needs is not simply to remove a psychic discomfort called loneliness, but to develop our potential for intimacy with ourselves, with nature, with God, and with fellow human beings.

Locating Group Support

Risks are minimized when we begin with small steps and gradually increase these steps as our confidence increases. Still, you may find it difficult to "go it alone." It may help to locate a support group. Other people are not obligated to solve your problems, and you are not obligated to solve theirs. But we can give each other support as we take steps necessary to solve our own.

This suggestion may startle you. If you are experiencing the isolation of loneliness, how can you locate such a group? Most people are unaware of many opportunities in their own community. I have often informed lifelong residents about opportunities they didn't know were available where they lived. Unless you know enough interested persons to form a support group of your own, become a researcher.

Pastors can usually tell you what is available in your community. Ask your own pastor first; then, if need be, ask others. Explain that you are looking for a support group that meets regularly for interaction to assist in your own personal growth. Sometimes congregations have such groups, although they are not usually advertised. Another place to investigate is your county or community mental health center or family counseling center. They may use the label "group therapy." If you shy away from the words *mental health* or *therapy,* let me assure you these opportunities are not for sick people, but for normal persons like yourself who want to grow.

Next make contact with the YMCA or YWCA in your community. If they are not conducting self-help groups themselves, they can often refer you to other possibilities. Then, if you are still without leads, get names of professional counselors in your community—perhaps through your county social welfare office—and ask these counselors where such opportunities are.

During this investigation you may come across more than one opportunity. If you have a choice, my suggestion is that you choose one whose leadership emphasizes support more than confrontation. I say this not because I am opposed to confrontation-style leadership, but because I do not know you and therefore cannot ascertain how you would respond to confrontation. You may also want to sit in with the group on a trial basis, if this is permitted, before deciding which is the best one for you. What you are looking for is a group that will provide you with a tangible backup for your efforts. Besides providing us with the encouragement we need to act, support groups also provide a "cushion" for the risks involved in the action we take.

In addition to support groups for self-help, specialized groups, usually of limited duration, may also be available in your community. These may be used to substitute for a support group, if you are unable to locate one that is satisfactory, or they may be used in addition to a support group. There are Marriage Encounter weekends—Catholic, Lutheran, Episcopal—with their follow-up support groups. Parent Effectiveness Training programs may be offered in churches or other community centers. If you are divorced, inquire about the nearest We Care or similar group. If you are a single parent, perhaps there is Parents Without Partners or a similar group in your community.

Specialized groups for a single person of mature years are usually oriented to business, professional, or political interests. Churches and other community agencies sponsor young adult programs and senior citizen groups.

If you are at least a potentially active person, investigate activities groups that specialize in such things as hiking, biking, backpacking, canoe trips, and cross-country skiing. Most communities also have periodic opportunities for religious retreats, workshops devoted to some aspect of personal growth, and conferences devoted to religious and psychological subjects. Such opportunities are usually announced in church bulletins or by public advertisement.

Besides providing the encouragement we need to act, support groups cushion us against risks. Special interest groups also provide opportunity for social experience, helping us develop our social sensitivities. They may become the source of ongoing personal relationships, since they bring together people with common interests.

The most important place for social involvement is the church. Most congregations are community-based and provide continuous fellowship. Faith provides a common base for interests and activities. The combination of the social with the spiritual and of activity with mission puts the church in a unique position as a resource for overcoming loneliness and developing intimacy.

Perhaps you say, "Not my church! There are too many complications in my congregation for it to minister to my needs." If this is the case I would suggest that you ask your pastor if these complications can be circumvented so you receive from your church the assistance you need. If this does not resolve the problem, perhaps you should find a congregation in which you *can* become involved. I would suggest that you stay within your own denomination if this is possible, since a big change in your religious orientation at this point could obstruct your primary concerns. There may be obstacles to leaving your congregation, particularly if it is a congregation with strong family ties. If so, determine your priorities and make your decision on this basis.

CHAPTER 10

CONCERN FOR OTHERS:

How the Lonely Can Help the Lonely

There are other lonely people, other hurting people, like yourself. Some have additional handicaps that add to their loneliness. Many people are institutionalized because of physical, mental, or social illnesses. Society tends to hide in institutions people whose handicaps are considered offensive or depressing. Loneliness abounds in institutions, from "rest homes" for the elderly to county jails. Many institutions need humanizing, and you can assist in this endeavor.

Other people belong to racial or economic subcultures that are not accepted by the mainline culture of our society. The alienation many of these people feel is a problem that belongs to all of us. Students who feel inadequate at school might profit from a tutor.

According to the commandment, "You shall love your neighbor as yourself," these hurting people are our concern. In the previous chapter we stressed meeting our own needs so we could love others. In this chapter we concentrate on loving others in terms of meeting *their* needs.

Freed Up to Reach Out

When we do not act directly to satisfy our needs, we tend to become preoccupied with our deprivations. Suffering can turn us inward as our psychic or physical pains absorb our attention. Preoccupation with our own discomforts produces a negative emotional state—a combination of anxiety, depression, and self-pity—that prevents us from empathizing with others in *their* needs. As we become increasingly insensitive to the pains of others, our world of concerns becomes very small. This state of mind constitutes genuine self-centeredness. We are preoccupied with our own needs, but do not act to satisfy them.

Preoccupation with one's pains is habit forming. Those with the habit are under the illusion that such preoccupation is tantamount to *doing* something. They feel the need to focus on—essentially to worry about—their problems, as though they were doing guard duty. Preoccupation provides pseudosecurity. By preserving their familiar, though miserable, mind-set, they feel safe. We tend to be at home with our habits, even our bad ones. Although such habitual preoccupation is difficult to break, we are not bound by it. We can be emancipated.

The misery associated with such negative preoccupation clearly indicates that this kind of turning inward does not meet one's needs. As social beings, we need to reach out to others—to center ourselves *beyond* ourselves. As human beings we cannot prosper unless our lives have meaning. This meaning has to be more than temporary fascination, some fleeting interest. It must center on something bigger than—something beyond—our own selves. This is why religious faith is pertinent to human fulfillment: it shifts the focus from ourselves to God, and through God to fellow human beings. The gospel provides a calling for our lives—a vocation to focus our energies.

This calling is also based on a human need—the need to contribute of ourselves, to contribute *ourselves,* to the greater good, the general welfare, of the human community. It is no coincidence that we feel satisfied when we help others. Those whose occupations permit them to apply their talents directly to human needs often feel fulfilled through their work.

When I heard clinical psychologist Miriam Polster speak on the subject of loneliness, she said she did not see how anybody could be lonely when she loved what she was doing. It was evident from her expression that she loved what *she* was doing. Not everybody is privileged to have satisfying occupations. If your job is not particularly meaningful, perhaps you should seek a change.

This may not always be possible, particularly in times of high unemployment or when specialized training can't be obtained. If your job lacks potential for fulfillment, you may meet at least some of your vocational needs through your avocation. Your local church congregation offers many meaningful activities and opportunities for creative endeavor. You may find that you perceive more opportunities for meaningful experience in your job when you are inwardly satisfied through involvement in service activities of the church.

We can grow in sensitivity to the needs and desires of others, especially by listening to their feelings. According to an American Indian saying, one can understand another only by walking in the other's moccasins. Listening is the way we get to know how it feels in the other's moccasins. We obtain a glimpse into another's inner world and begin to feel *with* him or her. Such empathy is a basis for both intimacy and healing.

The flow, the movement, is from ourselves outward as we move forward, respond to, reach out to another. As we have seen, we fear making these overtures in intimacy. We have mixed feelings about the developing ties that sharing creates. We fear rejection. We feel exposed and vulnerable. Our defense system is threatened. We wonder where intimacy will lead.

We need to take these fears seriously, since they confront us with important questions that need to be answered. But they need not control us or render us immobile, just as we need not be bound to preoccupation with our pains. We are called out of ourselves through our relationship with God. Our identity is not determined by momentary feelings, since in the midst of these we can visualize the outstretched arms of Jesus beckoning, "Come unto me!" It is one thing to be afraid; it is another to become bogged down by fear. Faith is the antidote to fear. By faith we can turn from our fears to reach out in sensitivity to the needs of others.

Beyond Our Own Needs

The commitment that is basic to our religious calling is noticeably lacking in many current self-help movements. In fact, some stress the opposite—that one is obligated primarily if not solely to oneself, and there is no commitment beyond the satisfaction of one's own needs. In an article significantly titled "The New Narcissism," Peter

Marin criticizes these human potential movements for their trend "toward a deification of the isolated self." He says such deification results in unconcern about the needs of others. "What disappears in this view of things is the ground of community, the felt sense of collective responsibility for the fate of each separate other." [5]

I recently completed a sabbatical exploring programs of this movement, the spirit of which is involved in most of our current psychotherapies. My conclusion is that Marin has overstated his case by painting all the variety within this movement with the same brush. There *are* differences: Carol Rogers is of another cut, for example, from Werner Erhard of Erhard Seminars Training (EST) fame.

But there remains an element of truth in Marin's criticism. In attempting to reverse the self-denial syndrome which has blocked so many from taking the necessary steps to meet their own needs, the human potential therapies tend to the other extreme. One can get the impression from their emphasis that only what *I want* is important, and the thought of sacrificing for others is largely missing. But sacrifice is fundamental to the Christian way: "Greater love has no man than this, that a man lay down his life for his friends" (John 15:13). To seek only one's own satisfaction "goes against our grain." Unless people have something that takes them beyond self-seeking, the values of the human potential movement are likely to be short-lived. The sense of meaning necessary for healthy living comes from being called into an identity beyond our own.

Transcendental meditation considers one of its strengths to be that it asks no commitment from its adherents beyond the effort it takes to meditate. Its benefit, therefore, is like that of a medicine or an exercise. It can be and is helpful to those who already have a commitment. For example, my involvement in these movements has been helpful in expanding my identity as a Christian. But these movements will not—can not—provide meaning and identity for those who lack them.

We are responsible to values beyond our own fulfillment. Commitment beyond our own satisfaction is basic to our *human* nature. The Christian message identifies this commitment as identification with Christ. As he gave himself for us, so we respond by giving ourselves to him, by participating in his mission. "For the love of Christ controls us, because we are convinced that one has died for all; therefore all have died. And he died for all, that those who live might live no longer for themselves but for him who for their sake died and was raised" (2 Cor. 5:14-15).

We Receive that We May Also Give

Some people are uncomfortable to be on the receiving end. Their sense of worth is based on being givers. Others resist giving. They are bargain hunters who always want to get, since their sense of worth is based on getting the "best of the deal." Both giving and receiving are fundamental to human fulfillment. We have emphasized the importance of being open to receive. In this chapter emphasis is on the importance of being willing to give.

Giving to others is good for us. But this is not the sole reason for giving. Giving is also a response to another's need. Another's need is sufficient reason for giving—a point Jesus illustrated in his parable of the good Samaritan. A Jew lay helplessly wounded by the side of the road. The ethnically alienated Samaritan was the only one who responded. The need of the victim was sufficient stimulus for his response.

Since the wounded man could offer nothing in return, the Samaritan was expressing Jesus' own formula for giving. "When you give a dinner or a banquet, do not invite your friends or your brothers or your kinsmen or rich neighbors, lest they also invite you in return, and you be repaid. But when you give a feast, invite the poor, the maimed, the lame, the blind, and you will be blessed, because they cannot repay you" (Luke 14:12-14). Giving is not calculating. The needs of the wounded, the poor, the maimed, the lame, and the blind are sufficient motivation.

Our most important gift is the giving of ourselves—our person. I hope by now—if not before—you see the worth of your person, even apart from your accomplishments and your talents. As there are many kinds of needs, so there are also many ways of helping. Each of these ways is a symbol of our concern—of our self-giving. Perhaps you or somebody you know has artistic or musical talents. When a man paints, he is sharing himself through his painting. It is his communication—his contribution. So also when a woman performs through music, she invests herself, her feelings and aspirations, with her talent. In a similar way all of our efforts are to a degree a representation of ourselves—a mode of self-giving—an art, a skill, a communication. They form the channels through which our need to contribute is satisfied.

Combining Our Efforts in Corporate Concern

We discussed the value of a support group to assist us in reaching out to others as a way of coping with our loneliness. So also when we reach out in response to another's needs, it is often beneficial to combine our efforts with those of others. Much of our response to human need is on a one-to-one basis, but in some situations combined efforts are more effective. One of the finest mental hospitals with which I am acquainted insists on a commitment from the family of a mentally disturbed person to assist its staff with the therapy before it will accept the patient. This obviously makes it difficult for the person whose family refuses to cooperate. Yet the amazing results of this hospital demonstrate the effectiveness of such cooperation.

We particularly need to work cooperatively when attempting to change the structures or procedures by which various sectors of our society operate. At times these structures themselves obstruct satisfaction of needs they are supposed to facilitate. This is why we try on occasion to effect changes in the laws and practices that govern our society and its institutions. To be effective in such efforts we usually need the power of corporate action. If you have concerns about human needs in our society, look for others who believe as you do and discuss with them possible courses of action.

In the areas of medical care, education, nutrition, corrections, housing, family relations, community relations, employment, alcohol and drugs, conservation, and pollution control, most communities have much room for improvement. Political or church groups already organized to assist in these improvements may be looking for additional support. Your involvement in action or service groups in whose programs you believe provides support these groups need to be effective.

Perhaps it bears repeating that we must bring our identity to these groups rather than seeking to find it in them. If we expect from such groups what they are not able to give, we will expose ourselves to disappointment and also negatively affect our involvement. There is, however, no clear cut division between contributing ourselves with our identity to these groups and seeking to find an identity through their activities, since our involvement in them may—and hopefully will—enhance the identity we already possess. If we are aware of this mutuality between contributing and receiving, it can be a constructive factor in our involvement.

Keeping Busy

In stressing this importance on service and action groups I might be giving the impression that the answer to loneliness is in keeping busy. Unfortunately, keeping busy is a way many people in our culture try to cope with their problems, including the problem of loneliness. They pour their energies into their many activities at the expense of their relationships to themselves, to nature, to God, and even to others. Although these activities involve them with others, their task-oriented approach protects them from the hazards of intimacy. Keeping busy is a form of escapism. On the other hand, involvement in activities directed at meeting the needs of others fulfills our own needs. Satisfaction comes from working with others on projects, from setting goals and achieving these goals, and from growing in our own effectiveness.

There may be temporary failures rather than achievements, frustrations rather than satisfactions, and diversity of opinion—even friction—regarding procedures. Yet these problems, so common to volunteer organizations, are also potential growing pains both for the group and for its members. Difficulties help keep us realistic (hopefully not pessimistic) and provide good material for reflection in the search for better ways. They help us accept our limits and learn to function within them.

Through the tenuous nature of our goals, we learn to appreciate the present as something meaningful in itself and not simply as a means to a future objective. Busy people tend to be future-oriented so the present moment is like the movement of a car on a trip—its only significance is in its speed and the direction in which it is moving. Fulfillment for future-minded people is reserved for the completion of the trip. Ironically, however, because of their future orientation, the end of the trip brings only fleeting satisfaction, since by that time they are already preparing for the next trip. Fulfillment is always beyond them.

Potential of the Present

Your involvement in service projects will obviously have a future dimension. You will plan and set goals. Yet the present moment is the source for your fulfillment. If you are open to this potential of the present, you are open to intimacy. You will be able to pause in the midst of your activities to smell the flowers.

Association with others in action or service activities is a positive by-product of our involvement. Friendships can develop from these associations. The activities also have value in themselves: working with others can be *fun*.

If you live alone, you are well aware of times that may be especially lonely, such as weekends and holidays. If you plan activities for these times, you are making an intelligent attempt to satisfy your own needs. If you involve yourself in activities whose goals center in concern for others, you are responding to your calling. There need be no conflict between these two courses of action. Together they live out the wisdom of the commandment to love your neighbor as yourself.

We have called loneliness a problem—and it is! But it is also an opportunity. Through exploring this problem we have discussed the entire scope of opportunities for human fulfillment. The translation of loneliness from problem to opportunity is aptly expressed by a woman who has lived alone through 12 years of widowhood:

> Lately I've been feeling that maybe loneliness is a human sensation given to us to drive us into relationship, even as hunger drives us to food and tiredness drives us to sleep. In that sense, it's a beautiful gift, for without loneliness to make us hurt, some of us would wall ourselves in and wither in our separateness. As I'm driven into relationship by my loneliness, life opens up to me again.[6]

This is *creative loneliness!*

Notes

1. Jonathan Braun, "The Struggle for Acceptance of a New Birth Technique," *Parade,* November 23, 1975, p. 17.

2. Edna Hong, *Turn Over Any Stone* (Minneapolis: Augsburg Publishing House, 1970), pp. 29-30.

3. William L. Roberts and Ann E. Roberts, *Factors in Lifestyles of Couples Married over Fifty Years,* Louisville, Ky.: Gerontological Society 28th Annual Scientific Meeting [1975], Doct. 26-30.

4. Grace Halsell, "The Viejos of Ecuador," *Braniff Place,* Vol. 4, No. 5, p. 4.

5. *Harper's Magazine,* October 1975, p. 48.

6. Char Meredith, "Sometimes I Feel Lonely," *Faith at Work,* August 1976, p. 32.